GUIDELINES FOR GROWING CHRISTIANS

by LeRoy Lawson

STANDARD PUBLISHING

Cincinnati, Ohio 18-39950

Unless otherwise noted, all Scripture quotations are taken from The New International Version, ©1978 by New York International Bible Society, and are used by permission.

Cover Photo by Comstock

Copyright ©1989. The STANDARD PUBLISHING Company, Cincinnati, Ohio. A division of STANDEX INTERNATIONAL Corporation. Printed in U.S.A.

Library of Congress Cataloging-in-Publication Data

Lawson, E. LeRoy, 1938-
  Guidelines for growing Christians / by LeRoy Lawson.
    p. 160
  Bibliography: p.
  ISBN 0-87403-520-1
  1. Christian life—1960-   I. Title.
BV4501.2.L3652   1989
248.8'4—dc19

TABLE OF CONTENTS

Where Do You Go After You've Arrived?

Philippians 3:12-16

I am a new Christian. Now what?
I've been born again. What's next?
I'm saved. For what?
I've been baptized. Is this all I need to do?
Have you ever wondered why God doesn't just pluck us out of the water of baptism and plunk us down in Heaven? What grief He would save us! What sins we would not commit, what a lot of repentance we could be spared, if only we didn't have to keep on living in this tempting world!

If only. . . . Yet these are questions no loving parent would raise about a newborn baby. The joy of new birth gives way quickly to the joy of growth. In fact, if the infant does not develop into the toddler and on to the child and then the adolescent and finally the adult, the celebration of the birth turns to mourning. New birth of itself means nothing if it is not followed by growth.

If you want to grow up as a Christian, this book is for you. You have arrived safely in the arms of God. You have experienced His love, His forgiveness and His acceptance, even though you have felt yourself unacceptable. You have arrived. Where do you go next?

This book is also for people like me, who have been in Christ for several years, but who seem to have reached a growth plateau. No measurable changes have occurred in recent years. For us, it's examination time, like an annual physical checkup, to see how our spiritual "organs" are functioning.

We'll begin with the apostle Paul, who made spiritual growth such an important theme in his writings—because it was so important to his personal life. Probably his most famous statement on the subject is the one we have taken as the basis of this chapter Philippians 3:12-16. It is so important to Paul that he repeats himself. Verse 12 introduces the theme, and verses 13 and 14 repeat it.

Look at verse 12. In it Paul indicates three building blocks of growth.

1. Look at his attitude: I haven't obtained—I'm not perfect.
2. Look at the energy he expends: I press on.
3. Look at the goal he has set before him: I take hold of that for which Christ took hold of me.

Verses 13 and 14 elaborate a little more, but they deal with the same things: attitude, energy, and goal. Building blocks so important to the great apostle must be essential for us as well, so we'll start our new spiritual development program right here, with an examination of our attitude, our energy output, and our goal in life. We'll change Paul's order a bit, moving the goal to first place so it can provide the motive for our attitude and energy.

The Goal: The Prize for Which God Has Called Us Heavenward in Christ Jesus

In verse 12 Paul admits that he has not "already been made perfect." In verse 15 he states that "all of us who are mature" should have the same view of things that he has. Perfect and mature are different English words to translate the same basic Greek word, teleios. Something becomes mature or perfect when it reaches the state in which it fulfills the purposes for which it was made. We Christians can be said to have achieved maturity or perfection, then, when we have become what God wants us to be. Jesus encourages us in His Sermon on the Mount to "be perfect, therefore, as your heavenly Father is perfect" (Matthew 5:48).

Our goal, then, is not simply to arrive at Heaven's door one day. It is to develop a God-like character; it is to be as fully human (by God's definition) as God is fully divine. It is to have grown into the person God had in mind when He made us. Here is how Paul states it:

> We proclaim him [Christ], admonishing and teaching everyone with all wisdom, so that we may present everyone perfect in Christ. —Colossians 1:28

Paul defines perfection (or maturity) as becoming like Christ:

> It was he [Christ] who gave . . . so that the body of Christ may be built up until we all reach unity in the faith and in the knowledge of the Son of God and become mature, attaining to the whole measure of the fulness of Christ. —Ephesians 4:11-13

For Paul, Christian growth is not some vague and distant dream. It has an immediate, personal, achievable goal. We know who Christ is and what Christ is like. We know who we are and what the distance between ourselves and Christ is. We can see, if our eyes are open and our attitude is right, what we must become.

You may be tempted to put this book down right now. If you are, you'll have lots of company. Among adults, talk of personal growth ranks pretty low on the list of desirables. We remember the growing pains we had as children; as adults we have discovered that there is never any growth without pain. ("No pain, no gain" my son the weight lifter tells me.) Pain is something we can do without—if growth requires it, we'll manage not to grow, thank you.

There will be others, though, hardy souls they, who won't be threatened by this talk of personal perfection. They aren't satisfied with second best and aren't pleased to find themselves mired in mediocrity. They want to grow. They echo Oliver Wendell Holmes in his poem, "The Chambered Nautilus":

> Build thee more stately mansions, O my soul,
> As the swift seasons roll!
> Leave thy low-vaulted past!
> Let each new temple, nobler than the last,
> Shut thee from heaven with a dome more vast,
> Till thou at length art free
> Leaving thine outgrown shell by life's unresting sea.

Do you remember this poem from your high-school English class? Generations of American kids have memorized at least this much of it, as idealistic teachers have done their best to instill in their students a desire to keep on developing even after they leave school. They hoped some of their students would do more than merely memorize; they dared to believe some of them would actually build more stately souls.

I wonder what they would have said to Jimmy Connors, the tennis pro who has done so much to bring America fame—for his brilliant maneuvers on the court and his uninhibited manners there and elsewhere. "Mature is a bad word," he has been quoted as saying. "I never want to grow up. I always want to stay the way I am."[1]

He'll get at least half of what he wants. He may not stay the way he is, but he certainly will not grow up—not without a change of attitude. Contrast his self-satisfaction with

Paul's eagerness to change. Paul is often called the great-est Christian who ever lived (a judgment that only God is qualified to make), yet he realizes that he still has some improvements to work on. Christ grasped him in his fa-mous encounter on the road to Damascus (Acts 9); now he wants to grasp Christ in return, to hold Him, to serve Him, to become like Him.

He keeps his goal ever before him, so that as an older man he can write this to Timothy:

> I have fought the good fight, I have finished the race, I have kept the faith. Now there is in store for me the crown of righteousness, which the Lord, the righteous Judge, will award to me on that day—and not only to me, but also to all who have longed for his appearing.
> —2 Timothy 4:7, 8

To the very end the goal is before him. He wants "to take hold of that for which Christ Jesus took hold" of him. He wants "to win the prize for which God has called" him "heavenward in Christ Jesus." He strives for "the crown of righteousness" which the Lord will award him at the end. His is a goal-oriented, God-directed life.

Attitude: Humble Forgetfulness

At first blush, Paul seems an unlikely example to use on the subject of growth. He strikes us as a "man who has everything." Philippians 3:4-6 contains his catalog of achievements. See also Acts 26:5; Galatians 1:14. He be-longed to the right clubs, held the proper opinions, out-paced his competitors, worked harder, served better and lasted longer than the rest. He was the leader of the pack. If he had never met Jesus, he could have retired from active duty with easy satisfaction. He was the best.

So it appears to us. But Paul knows better. When he came face to face with the Son of God, he became a changed man. He realized that everything he had ever been or achieved amounted to nothing. "I consider them [all his accomplishments] rubbish," he writes (Philippians 3:7, 8), comparing what he now has in Christ with everything else that once was his. Before God, he has nothing to boast about. So he forgets "what is behind" (Philippians 3:13).

What Paul says of himself we must all say, if we hope to grow in Christ. Some believers come into church boasting of "what is behind" in their lives. They are leaders in their community, teachers in their field. They are used to having people pay attention to them. They can't adjust to the fact that in the body of Christ, a great one in the world is "just one of us." Titles don't count, money doesn't count, fame doesn't count in the church. We are all just fellow sinners, trusting the grace of God to save us. If you have a lot in your past to boast about, forget it!

On the other hand, if you have much in your past to be ashamed of, forget that too. Too many people live in dread that they will be found out. Before they came to Christ they were guilty of various kinds of sin. They don't want to bring shame on themselves now, or embarrass the church, so they keep a low profile in the hope that their history won't surface. They haven't yet realized that it doesn't matter whether their past is ever discovered or not.

Forget the past. Be humble enough to put away your current mask of perfection. Everybody has a past; all have sinned. What matters is not what you were, but what you are becoming. So long as your focus is on yesterday, you can't grow. So forget it.

One more word. You must also forget past injuries. Sure, some people have hurt your feelings. They have insulted you, or slighted you, or treated you unjustly. If you want to grow up, there is one thing you must do about all these injustices. You must forget them. That's right, forget them. If you dwell on them, rehearsing them again and again in your mind, calling them up again every time you see the one who has hurt you, you are letting your life be dominated by someone else. For your own sake, you must forget the past. It is time to grow up.

So this must be your attitude. Let go of the past. Come to the Lord empty. Humbly. You haven't yet taken hold of everything the Lord has in store for you. He can't give it to you if you are already full. So forget.

And if you become discouraged with your progress, get ahold of one of those PBPGHFWMY buttons and wear it with pride. "Please be patient; God hasn't finished with me yet." It's OK to admit you're not perfect. In fact, you must admit it, if you want to reach Christlikeness.

Energy: Straining, Pressing On

This is the order: First, decide you want to become like Christ. That's your goal.

Then let your past be your past. With humility, admit that you haven't attained maturity. Give up your pride, your guilt, your resentment. Offer yourself to God empty-handed. Then He can do something with you.

Finally, realize that there is nothing casual about growing up. Remember: No pain, no gain. Give yourself to your cause without reservation. As Paul puts it, keep on "straining" toward what is ahead, "press on toward the goal." Throw all your energy into it.

In our church is a young man I really admire. He is a triathlon competitor. He puts himself through the most grueling training in order to compete in a swimming, biking, and running marathon. It strikes me as somewhat insane to punish the body as much as Gary punishes his, just to earn the privilege of punishing it even more in competition with other crazy people. Yet I admire him. He is straining to win a goal. His dedication is bringing out the best in him. Even a non-athlete like me can see the difference. He has lost excess weight. He has tightened his sagging muscles. His eyes are brighter, his smile is quicker, his overall attitude more positive. He's in control of his body, and it glows. He's changing for the better, and he likes it.

You can change for the better, too, in spite of the fact that most people think such change is impossible. You must not listen to them. They are wrong. In the years of my ministry I have observed some radical transformations. You can grow. You can realize your God-given potential. As we have seen, you need a goal, you need the right attitude, and then you need to apply your energy!

> For a man's ways are in full view of the Lord,
> and he examines all his paths.
> The evil deeds of a wicked man ensnare him;
> the cords of his sin hold him fast.
> He will die for lack of discipline,
> led astray by his own great folly.   —Proverbs 5:21-23

As a public high-school teacher and then later as a college professor, I observed many promising young students who should have had brilliant careers in their chosen fields; but some of them settled into comfortable mediocrity or even fell into failure. Their goals were not wrong and their attitudes were acceptable, but their energy levels were too low. They would not strain; they did not press on toward their goals.

Altogether too often the same affliction has stunted the growth of young Christians. They started well, but their oomph gave out. Rather than talk about anyone I know personally, let me recount the biography of Fyodor Dostoyevsky, the peerless Russian author. Son of a surgeon, blessed with a gifted mind, Dostoyevsky became famous at twenty-five for his first novel, *Poor Folk.* Reveling in his success, the author took to drink and partying, and carelessly criticizing the czarist government. While in a St. Petersburg jail serving time for his anti-government activity, he was nearly executed, but was spared at the last possible moment by an edict from the czar.

Instead of death, he was exiled to Siberia for four years. The only book he was allowed there was the New Testament, which he devoured. It led him to new life. He discovered that Christ could raise the sinner, even one like him. After his release he wrote a woman that "there is nothing more beautiful, more profound, more sympathetic, more reasonable, more manly, and more perfect than Christ." He gave his heart to the Lord.

But he never seemed to grow as a Christian. He was careless in his worship attendance, undisciplined in his Bible study, and bereft of a more mature Christian who could take him under his wing and teach him how to live the Christian life. He began to drink too much again. His wife slowly died of consumption. He had an affair. He gave way to compulsive gambling and lost so much money that he was all but bankrupt. His writing became gloomy, and so did his personal affairs. He died penniless.

Dostoyevsky's goal was right. His attitude of humble forgetfulness was right. But he did not press on. He failed to discipline himself to win the prize.

So far I have made it sound as if you have to do all the work yourself in Christian growth. That's because I have selected only one passage to study.

I could have selected another one that would have given a more balanced picture. Here it is:

Continue to work out your salvation with fear and trembling, for it is God who works in you to will and to act according to his good purpose.   —Philippians 2:12, 13

Look carefully at what Paul says here. You must work out your salvation with fear and trembling. God is working in you. You must work even as God works. That's it. It's a partnership. You do what you can; God adds the rest.

An incident in one of the tidal rivers near New York City shows how this works. The building of a bridge was interrupted because a sunken ship at the bottom of the river was in the way. Divers put chains about the derelict, and tugs tried to dislodge it. It wouldn't budge.

A young technical-school graduate asked for the privilege of trying to remove it. The chief of operations skeptically demanded to know what the novice would propose to do.

His solution was simple. He took the flatboats in which the workers had brought granite from Vermont and, when the tide was out, fastened them to the derelict. Then when the Atlantic tide began to come in, it lifted the flatboats — and with them the sunken ship. He had merely harnessed the infinite energy of the ocean.

So the energy we use in growing up in Christ comes from two sources: ourselves, and the infinite power of the Lord. We discipline ourselves and allow the Lord to discipline us. We work and allow Him to work through us.

Here's the rub, though. At first, this new partnership in life rebuilding seems pretty terrific. We drop a little sin here, another one there; then we congratulate ourselves on our progress—and quit progressing. Some of the things the Lord seems to want us to do pinch too much, so we shut Him out and stop the work.

C. S. Lewis in *Mere Christianity* tells us how this works, borrowing a parable from his mentor in the faith, George MacDonald. He says to imagine yourself as a living house. You invite God to come in and rebuild the house. You like what He does at first—He fixes the drains and stops the leaks in the roof. So far so good. Then He begins knocking things around and He hurts you a bit. He has done everything you wanted—but He keeps going. He knocks out a wall here and there, throws out a new wing here, adds an extra floor there, runs up towers, makes courtyards. "You thought you were going to be made into a decent little cottage, but he is building a palace. He intends to come and live in it himself."[2]

No, you don't have to strain and struggle impossibly to make yourself into a mature Christian. You are in partnership with God; He wants to help you. But beware—when He is your partner, He'll keep going until He makes you perfect, mature, whole, complete. I challenge you—don't stop Him. He's building you into a palace.

Keep on growing.

CHAPTER ONE

The Bigger They Are . . .

Philippians 2:1-11

My attitude should be the same as Christ's?
Impossible! He's the Son of God. I'm just a human being.
"In humility consider others better" than myself?
Wrong! In this "dog-eat-dog" world, the meek aren't the
blessed—they are the battered.
Look to the interests of others?
Not I! I have enough to do looking out for myself. Let
others look to their own interests.

What should we make of this passage, Philippians 2:1-
11? The apostle Paul insists that we must "do nothing out
of selfish ambition or vain conceit." He says we should "in
humility" consider others better than ourselves. Can we
take him seriously?

Your attitude, Paul insists, should be the same as that of
Christ Jesus. And what did Christ do? The same thing that
Paul did (Philippians 3:13, 14), but on an even more mag-
nificent scale. He forgot what was behind and strained

toward what was ahead. He "did not consider equality with God something to be grasped"; but He "humbled himself," left Heaven itself behind, and became a servant. He obeyed God even to the point of dying on a cross. It is this attitude that we Christians are to adopt.

What can we say of such an order?

Nearly Impossible

We begin by admitting that it is nearly impossible. Such humility does not come to us naturally.

Listen to some of today's stars. They seem to have everything—everything, that is, except humility. "I'm the straw that stirs the drink; it all comes back to me," boasts Reggie Jackson of New York Yankeedom. Howard Cosell, the sports broadcaster everybody loves to hate, doesn't need anyone else's applause. He provides his own. "I really believe I'm the best. My relationship with the men who play the games is probably unparalleled in this country." Joan Kennedy isn't far behind Cosell and Jackson in her self-appreciation: "I have talent. I know I've still got my looks. I know I've got all these terrific things going for me. I mean . . . you're talking to, I think, one of the most fascinating women in this country."

Robert Russell, who is my source for these self-congratulations, also tells of the time a few years back when his son interviewed a college basketball star on assignment for his grade-school class. Young Russell asked the All-American who became Rookie of the Year in the National Basketball Association, "How old were you when you realized you were better than everybody else?"

"Oh, about sixth grade," the athlete seriously answered.[1]

How do you teach somebody who is better than anybody else? Russell's article also quotes Mickey Rooney, who answers this question: "I'm fifty-eight years in the theatre. Nobody gives me instructions." That's how you teach the proud—you don't!

If we had time we'd discuss the incredibly mixed careers of Rooney, Kennedy, and others whose public posture radiates such supreme self-confidence. Their biographies give the lie to their boasts. They make me think of a novel by Stella Benson entitled *I Pose.* Her opening sentence reads, "Sometimes I pose, but sometimes I pose as posing." That in turn reminds me of T. S. Eliot's famous poem, "The Love Song of J. Alfred Prufrock," in which he speaks of preparing a face to meet the faces that we meet day by day. You can't be quite sure, when you first meet someone, whether you have actually met the person or the mask the person is wearing that day. Similarly, Muhammad Ali's boast, "I am the greatest," or the equally arrogant sounds of stars and politicians may not express the real feelings of the speakers. They may be the bragging noises of inwardly scared children trying to frighten away a boogeyman.

Psychologists have long been fascinated by what one of them, Alfred Adler, called the inferiority complex. He observed that we all grow up with feelings of inferiority. That is because we started out inferior. We were smaller than adults, weaker, not as knowledgeable, not as skilled. To feel inferior when we are children is OK—because we are. To carry those feelings of inferiority into maturity is not OK. If by the time you are an adult you are still inhibited by your feelings of inadequacy, Adler calls these feelings an inferiority complex. It spells trouble.

All of this you know. You know also that many people try to overcome their inner fears of inferiority by pretending superiority. They brag, they ride over others, they put on a mask of absolute self-confidence so their fears won't be discovered. Perhaps we can't tell whether they're pretending or not.

The problem is that even when they are only pretending to know everything, they limit their capacity to learn. Who is able to teach them? If they claim to be already at the top of their field, how can they admit that anyone knows enough to instruct them?

Here we need to heed the wisdom of this ancient Proverb:

Pride goes before destruction, a haughty spirit before a
fall.   —Proverbs 16:18

This one isn't to be ignored, either:

Whoever gives heed to instruction prospers and blessed
is he who trusts in the Lord.   —Proverbs 16:20

You won't hear the Lord's instructions if you are convinced that you are already the best; your haughty spirit is
preparing you for a fall.

According to one of the hundreds of tales told about the
Greek philosopher Socrates, a young man presented himself in order to learn the art of conversation. As they were
becoming acquainted, however, he talked so much that
Socrates said he could not accept him as a pupil without a
double fee. "Why do you charge me double?" the surprised young man asked him.

"Because I must teach you two things. The one how to
hold your tongue, and the other how to speak."

In the same vein Paul writes to his friends in Philippi,
"In humility consider others better than yourselves." If
you will do this, you can learn from them all.

What does he mean by humility? We today are afraid to
admit that somebody else may be better than we are at
something, or afraid to forget ourselves and our interests
lest we get hurt. But forgetting ourselves is exactly what
humility is all about. Remember what Jesus said about
becoming like little children? His disciples demanded to
know who would be the greatest in the kingdom of
Heaven. He answered by calling a little child into the center of the group.

I tell you the truth, unless you change and become like
little children, you will never enter the kingdom of
heaven. Therefore, whoever humbles himself like this
child is the greatest in the kingdom of heaven.
                                        —Matthew 18:3, 4

What's so good about a child? The next time you have a chance spend some time watching a little one at play. You'll discover what Jesus is talking about. When a child is playing, really playing, he is totally absorbed in his project. If you let him see that you are watching, you'll ruin it. Then he'll begin to act for you. But if he is alone and really into whatever he is doing, you'll see that he is concentrating completely. He has no consciousness of time, no self-consciousness. He has forgotten himself. That's humility.

Clearly Necessary

Humility is clearly necessary, if we are to grow. Ben Franklin said he learned this lesson as a young man. He had been visiting the famous preacher Cotton Mather who was showing him out of the house when Franklin hit his head on the low beam. Mather had told him to stoop, but the words registered too late to save Franklin a bump on his pate. Then Mather added insult to injury: "You are young and have the world before you; STOOP as you go through it, and you will miss many hard thumps." When he was an old man of seventy-eight, Franklin still recalled this advice, adding that he often thought of it when he saw the misfortunes people brought on themselves by carrying their heads too high.[2]

To help such people in the church at Rome, the apostle Paul wrote,

For by the grace given me I say to every one of you: Do not think of yourself more highly than you ought, but rather think of yourself with sober judgment, in accordance with the measure of faith God has given you.

—Romans 12:3

Remember what Jesus said about becoming like a child. To be child-like is to be humble and teachable like a child, knowing we are not yet mature. It is not to be childish, which often suggests being selfish and irrational, or pretending to be somebody we aren't.

Several years ago Joy and I took a group of college students on a study tour of Europe. For six weeks we toured through portions of twelve countries, visiting cathedrals, museums, and sites of historical significance. My task, of course, was to help them grasp something of the historical and cultural importance of the sites we visited. One of the students was quite bright and quick to speak. He had no doubt of his intelligence and no little doubt about mine, so he did not hesitate to share with the group the benefits of his vast knowledge. When he was right, I let him talk. When he wasn't I tried to correct him without embarrassment. My wife, however, became increasingly exasperated until she could contain herself no longer. Taking him aside one day, she told him, "My husband is a very good teacher. You do not know it all. He could even teach you something if you would let him. Why don't you be quiet and let him talk for a change?"

When she told me about the conversation later, I thanked her for her confidence (which I did not entirely share) and for the favor she did all of us. From then on, there was much less tension in the group and, I hope, even my young expert picked up an occasional stray bit of information he did not already possess. He was, in fact, quite an able young man. But he had one thing left to learn—he had not yet mastered the art of stooping.

Sam Rayburn, for many years the Speaker of the House of Representatives in Washington, used to admonish young congressmen, "When you're talking, you ain't learning." I am frequently taken aback when I listen to certain dogmatic, self-confident persons holding forth at great length on this or that Scriptural subject. They sound so sure of themselves; they seem to think they know so much. I have spent my life studying the Scriptures and can't claim to know all they confidently declare. Then I realize, if I listen to them long enough, that they don't have it all together. They're so busy talking that they "ain't learning." They are pretending to be something they aren't.

I have a friend who suffered an emotional collapse when he was in his mid-fifties. He had had a very successful career. He had been at the top of his profession. He had received honors of every kind and had become accustomed to having his every order obeyed. Then he changed professions. Within a year he was on the verge of nervous collapse. His friends had warned him ahead of time. They had told him he was used to playing God in his former career. In his new one, he would be challenged and treated like a normal human being. They had asked him whether he could take it. He had assured them he could.

He couldn't. He wouldn't. He had to resign his position for his sanity's sake. He returned to his former profession, where once again he could play God.

Humility—how can I say this any more strongly—humility is not a luxury. It is an absolute necessity. Without it you can't grow; without it you won't learn; without it even God can't do what He wants to do with you. So "do nothing out of selfish ambition or vain conceit, but in humility consider others better than yourselves."

Finally Rewarding

Then you will discover that humility has its own rewards, and they are great.

For one thing, God can bless you. One of Jesus' most famous parables is about two men who went up to the temple to pray. One was a Pharisee, a most righteous man. Everybody looked up to him and others like him as examples of good religious behavior. They admired him. So did he. "God, I thank you that I am not like all other men—robbers, evildoers, adulterers—or even like this tax collector." His prayer was an exercise in self-congratulation.

The other man was a tax collector, hated by his fellow citizens and not much appreciated by himself. "God, have mercy on me, a sinner."

Yet, surprise of surprises, Jesus says that the humble tax collector, not the self-righteous Pharisee, is the one God justifies. Then He adds the stinger: "For everyone who exalts himself will be humbled and he who humbles himself will be exalted" (Luke 18:9-14).

The Bible makes itself very clear. God wants to bless people. But He can't give growth or improvement to people who are already satisfied with themselves. This is why Jesus has such surprising things to say in the Sermon on the Mount:

Blessed are the poor in spirit,
for theirs is the kingdom of heaven.
. . . .
Blessed are the meek
for they will inherit the earth.

We aren't used to such talk. "Blessed are the rich," we say. "Blessed are the tough, the aggressive, the proud." "If you expect to get ahead, you've got to think of yourself first."

Yet Jesus' Beatitudes have a ring of truth to them, don't they?

A missionary in India was about to board a train when he asked the Indian gentleman standing beside him, "Are you going on this train?"

"No, I cannot go, for there are only third-class carriages on it."

"I am going," the missionary told him.

"Yes," his acquaintance said, "you can go, for you are a religious man. If you go first-class, it does not exalt you; and if you go third-class it does not degrade you. You are above these distinctions. But I have to keep up my prestige."[3]

This man will never inherit the earth—he can't even accept a third-class seat on a train.

Humility makes it possible for you to go anywhere the train goes, enjoy everything good, appreciate all that God has made. It means that, like Paul, you can be poor or wealthy, you can have nothing or an abundance, you can live like a pauper or like a king, and it doesn't affect you. What freedom you have! What blessings you receive!

And in the end, you discover that while others have just been passing through their limited tenure on earth, you have absorbed and enjoyed so much that you are ready to enjoy the next life even more. Since you don't know it all yet, you are open to learn. Since you don't have much, you are eager to receive whatever God has to give you. Since you aren't self-important, you are free to hobnob with anybody, high or low on the social scale. Since you aren't perfect and you know it, you don't have to pretend to be. You aren't uptight, since you don't have to prove anything to anybody in order to keep up your pose of superiority. Oh, how free you are to grow!

Did you watch *Backstairs at the White House* when the series was on television? I did and I enjoyed it so much I purchased the book on which it was based. It traces the experiences of two chief maids there, Maggie and her daughter Lillian, through half a century of service. There is a touching moment of truth when Mercer, who served as butler through those same years, is preparing wistfully to take his leave.

"A man stays better than half his life in a place," Mercer says, "then suddenly one day it comes on him, he don't belong."

Maggie corrects him. "Oh, you belong ... the Pres-'dents, their families, they jus' the tenants, we the ones lived here ... "[4]

There's wisdom in her words. The big shots who moved in and moved out with the elections were indeed just tenants. They didn't own the place. They didn't even really know the place. The humble servants, without whom the White House couldn't function and the Presidents couldn't officiate—they inherited the place. Theirs was the kingdom.

Jesus understood this truth better than anybody else. Paul says He lived in Heaven itself, but gave it all up so that He could mingle with and serve people of every class and kind on earth. He who had been king became servant.

But notice: that's not the end of the story. Because of His humility, "therefore God exalted him to the highest place and gave him the name that is above every name."

God lifts up the humble. He always has.

Do you want to grow? Then let your attitude "be the same as that of Christ Jesus who . . . humbled himself."

Discussion Starters for Small Groups

Do you agree or disagree with the following statement from chapter one: "Humility makes it possible for you to go anywhere . . . , enjoy everything good, appreciate all that God has made"?

In what way does the competitive spirit of our society make it difficult to cultivate a spirit of true humility? Give specific examples from various areas of endeavor—business, athletics, etc.

How can you look after both your own interests and the interests of others? What do you do if there is a conflict of interests?

How are humility and unity related?

How does Philippians 2:1-11 say we are to demonstrate humility?

How would your life be different if you consistently followed the example of Jesus in Philippians 2:5-11?

CHAPTER TWO

What Does Forgiveness Have to Do With Anything?

Matthew 18:21-35

Forgiveness is the answer to the child's dream of a miracle by which what is broken is made whole again, what is soiled is again made clean. —Dag Hammarskjold[1]

In the last chapter we studied humility, without which spiritual growth is impossible. Now we turn our attention to an equally essential building block, forgiveness. Jesus actually ties forgiveness to salvation, teaching that unless we forgive others, God will not forgive us: Matthew 18:21-35; 6:12-15; 7:1-5.

When we think about this subject, we quickly line up with Jesus. Forgiveness is so important that when we say someone has a Christian spirit, we mean that he has enough of Christ in him to forgive injury. (He is like Jesus on the cross who asked God to forgive His murderers—a generosity of spirit that still amazes even the most charitable.) If one has a Christian spirit he doesn't hold a grudge, he doesn't get even, he hastens to restore broken relationships.

Peter asks, "Lord, how many times shall I forgive?" (Matthew 18:21). Jesus' answer exposes the pettiness of the question. The true spirit of forgiveness does not keep score. You keep on forgiving, remembering how much God has forgiven, you.

Peter does not ask, but we must, "Whom shall I forgive?" Most of us practice selective grace. We tolerate some of our associates, actually go so far as to forgive a few of them, but have no compunction against vigorously judging the rest. Yet the Bible teaches that forgiveness, which does not keep score on the number of times it offers itself to a brother also refuses to keep score on the number of brothers or others it forgives. It adopts the forgiving attitude in general; it refuses to play favorites.

Whom then should we forgive?

We Begin by Forgiving God

It sounds strange to speak of forgiving God, doesn't it? I do not mean to imply that God ever does wrong. He does not. But He does allow some events that are tragic and agonizing, and sometimes we are tempted to blame Him for that. When I say we must forgive God, I mean we must cleanse our minds and hearts of any tendency to blame Him who is blameless.

Who actually says, "I'll never forgive God for this"? Unfortunately, many people do. In my ministry many troubled souls have told me that they could never forgive God for what they felt He had done to them. More, however do not blame God in so many words, but they mean the same thing as they grumble about their bad "luck" or the heavy load "circumstances" have forced them to carry in life. So they banish God from their lives, certain that He (or "life") has done them wrong. They'll show Him. They certainly will never forgive Him.

Their spirit of revenge reminds me of Peppermint Patty in a *Peanuts* comic strip. With impressive architectural skill she has constructed a magnificent sand castle, laboring over it until her high standards are satisfied. Then, when she has almost completed it, an ocean wave rolls in and wipes out her masterpiece. She sulks about it for several minutes, then asks Charlie Brown, "How do you get even with an ocean?"

You don't, of course. Neither do you get even with the tides of life that wipe out so many cherished dreams. There is no guarantee against tragedy or suffering on this planet. Since it is the lot of all men to suffer, every person must choose how he will react to it. He can try to get even with the ocean, or he can rise above his setback to build another castle, this time on higher ground.

I was in England recently for a college board meeting. I had just arrived when I was handed a message from my secretary in the States. She had called to tell me about infants in two of our church families. The first was only a week old and had just undergone surgery for a bowel obstruction. The operation was scheduled for the morning of my departure, so I had asked Judy to call to let me know what happened. She reported that the surgery was a success, but the doctors had informed the young parents that their newborn son was a victim of Down's syndrome. His mental future was limited.

Another tragedy struck on the day I left for England. The three-month-old son of another young couple was dead, the victim of sudden infant death syndrome, often called "crib death." Suddenly, inexplicably, the baby stopped breathing.

My days in England were clouded by my concern for these parents. How were they taking these blows? Was our church ministering to them? What would I say when I returned? As if God were preparing me for my return, He ministered to my grief through two special friends. Four of us ministerial and professional colleagues were scheduled for a tour from Birmingham to Edinburgh. When I shared my news from home with them, two of them quietly began telling me of their own stories. One had lost an infant son in the early months of his life; the other had a seventeen-year-old son so profoundly retarded that he could not recognize his own parents.

Both men had suffered deeply through their sons' tragedies. Yet they were both ministers of the good news of
Jesus Christ. They did not pretend to fully understand
everything in God's grand design, but they had experienced His love through their losses and trusted God's benevolence to care for their loved ones. Their "castles" had
been destroyed or damaged by life's cruel waves, but they
had not gone through life blaming God or getting even
with their ocean. They had grown in the quiet strength
that flowed from them into this troubled minister. I don't
need to tell you how much they helped me prepare for my
return home.

Back in Arizona I discovered that both of our young
couples had found the peace of God. The newborn boy
may be afflicted with Down's syndrome, but he will grow
up in a home saturated with love and guided by faith in
the God of love. The parents who lost their little boy had
already begun to thank God for the good that they were
uncovering in their plight. They were trusting the Lord to
care for their son, now that they no longer could. His
several weeks of life here had been a struggle; they
learned that his body had been wracked with problems,
from which he has now been rescued.

His mother asked me to read this letter to the members
of our church. It expresses how she and her husband have
come to terms with their "wave":

> On behalf of Tony and myself, we would like to thank
> each and every one of you for your friendship and
> prayers. When something like this happens, you always
> ask, "Why?" But with your strength and the Lord we
> know. We don't know what caused S.I.D.S. (sudden
> infant death syndrome) to take our son's life, but we do
> know this: God does know best! He needed His little
> angel. We're just thankful that He did loan him to us
> while He did. We know He does love us to let us be able
> to love our son while we had him.

It still hurts, knowing he's gone. But we know he's not gone forever. We will be with him again one day soon. Just knowing that makes the pain subside and makes life's troubles easier to bear. But your friendship and prayers made our loss easier to handle and accept. Thank you for everything you have done for us.

These young parents join multitudes of Christians who have found peace in the most tragic circumstances. They stand out from the masses of people who can't accept what life does to them. They stand with Christians everywhere who find victory in what the world calls defeat. There are enough such Christians to encourage all of us to be like them.

Let me tell you about the Bittermans, for example. On March 7, 1981, Charles Bitterman's body was found propped up on the front seat of a bus in Bogota, Colombia. It was blindfolded. It had a hole in the chest where a bullet had penetrated the heart. A red and black guerrilla army flag was beside the body, so the world would know who was responsible for this death.

Bitterman was a missionary with the Wycliffe Bible Translators. He had been working to give Colombian Indians the Bible in their own language. Just twenty-five years before he was martyred in this mission cause, five other missionaries had been massacred by the Auca Indians of that country.

What if Charles were your son? How would you accept the news of his brutal death? After all, he was in Colombia to do the Lord's work. Why did the Lord allow him to die? And in such a ghastly way? Could you forgive the Lord?

The Bittermans did. They did more: they flew to Colombia with a gift of ten thousand dollars their friends had raised to buy an ambulance for the Colombian Indians. The Bogota paper editorialized:

The family of the . . . linguist . . . has eloquently demonstrated that the imperishable principles of Christianity have not been lost. . . . To respond to such an inconceivable monstrosity of a crime by donating an ambulance is to interpret in a very beautiful fashion the lesson to love your neighbor.

The examples could be multiplied, but these are enough to establish the point. Without forgiving others, including God, you cannot grow. You choose the attitude with which you respond to the waves that drown your castles. You choose to hate, you choose to be bitter, you choose vengeance. But in so choosing, you hurt yourself most of all. You shut out the mercy of God. You keep Him from turning your tragedy into triumph. He wants to do you good (Romans 8:28), but your hard heart prevents Him.

You Must Also Forgive Your Parents

The call to forgiveness is a hard word for bitter people to hear. Their parents did them wrong, and they can't forget. They were abused children, suffering physical or psychological damage. They carry the scars their parents inflicted. Even worse, they let their feelings about their parents dictate their moods, choices, and attitudes far into adulthood. They think of themselves as mature, but in their refusal to leave home emotionally they remain childish. They will never grow up until they can accept their parents as the flawed human beings they were—and perhaps still are—and forgive them for their imperfect performance as parents.

Joyce Landorf's incisive book *Irregular People* should be required reading for anybody suffering at the hands of parents. She explains that many, many of us have what she calls "irregular people" in our lives. These are persons who are important to us, who matter a great deal to us, in fact, but who seem to have a gift for hurting us. Very often one's irregular person is a parent. What can we do about such a person? Landorf's conclusion, unsurprisingly, is the same as Jesus'. We can forgive.

She quotes her friend Chuck Swindoll on the subject of

forgetting injuries against us. Swindoll refers to three Scriptures that are indispensable:

1. Refuse to keep score (1 Corinthians 13:5);
2. Be bigger than any offense (Psalm 119:165);
3. Do not harbor a judgmental attitude (Matthew 7:1-5).

He then encourages his readers to focus on God, not humanity, as they determine to forget. By God's grace, it is possible for us to forgive and to forget.[2]

These are good principles. You can't grow unless you resolve to be bigger than anything anybody can do to you. You can't really be critical of your parents until you have outgrown them!

Have your parents done you wrong? How many times? What's the score? If you know the score, you are still judging, still thinking backwards, still locked up in your childhood. Only through forgiving them can you be set free.

I know this is difficult advice. I wouldn't offer it if I knew any other course that leads to growth, but there isn't any other. Mahatma Gandhi, quoting the Sanskrit, gave his followers this wise advice: "Forgiveness is the ornament of the brave." Only the brave grow up.

When you think about it, what right does a person have to expect anybody else, especially parents, to be perfect? When did that person achieve his own perfection, from which lofty perch he can sit in judgment on others? I like Paul Tournier's insight: "Accepting one's life means also accepting the sin of others which causes us suffering, accepting their nerves, their reactions [which I just mistyped as rejections, also something we must accept], their enthusiasms, and even their talents and qualities by means of which they outshine us."[3] Forgiveness means accepting others completely, accepting their weaknesses and faults, their strengths and virtues.

We have many laughs about what terrible things my parents did to me. I suffer from a small stature, a large nose, a bad ear, two bad eyes, a receding forehead, and sundry other deficiencies my children delight in describing. Further I am afflicted with asthma and hay fever triggered by allergic reactions to just about everything. I can trace some of these liabilities through my father's lineage, and the rest of them I can blame on my mother's people. Frankly, my parents should never have united to make me; they were genetically a bad mix. I have sneezed and wheezed my way through life because of them. Oh, how I have suffered because they made me!

In addition, I bear some pretty obvious scars on my psyche because of my parents' divorce. They also are guilty of some bad judgments from time to time.

To be certain, I have a pretty solid case against my parents. Now, what should I do with the evidence?

Burn it. The case is closed anyway, since I have long since accepted my parents for what they are and forgiven them for any mistakes they made. And as for my wheezes and sneezes, what person among us does not have some physical liability? Are my mother and father to be blamed? Of course not—not for my physical shortcomings nor for anything they may have done against me. I left that behind when I made up my mind to leave my childhood in the past and assume responsibility for myself. To become an adult one must forgive the forces of his childhood.

You Must Also Forgive Friends and Acquaintances

The acceptance granted to the realities of life and to parents is also extended to other people—friends, acquaintances, other family members and loved ones. I was thinking recently about my friends, about whom I can become pretty sentimental. What a loyal bunch they are! I suppose that I don't have a single friend whom I have not had to forgive for something at some time or other. Neither, on the other hand, have they been able to keep me in their affection without having to forgive me! My friends and I are living proof that there is no abiding friendship without forgiveness. People who can't forgive must be pretty lonely.

There is a woman in Chattanooga, Tennessee, who is a good/bad example of a failure to forgive. A judge there has ordered the eighty-four-year-old's telephone pad locked to keep her from further annoying a man she has harassed for the last forty-five years. The trouble began when her dog jumped from behind the hedges of her yard and nipped the heel of her paperboy. He reported the incident to the Humane Society. The dog was kept under observation for a few days, then returned to its owner.

Then her campaign began. Every day, up to ten times a day, the demented woman called the teenage paperboy. She kept it up after he married. She kept it up after children came, so that he and his wife had to prevent the children from answering the phone so they wouldn't have to listen to her profanity. In 1965 she was ordered to the county penal farm (she was making about ten calls a day then) for four months. When she was released, she picked up where she had left off. The judge now says that if she doesn't stop, he'll order her back to the work farm.

For forty-five years she has allowed a simple offense to dominate her life and rob another's life of peace. Her bitterness has literally driven the woman crazy. (What we so cavalierly label mental illness is thought by some psychologists to be at base a moral problem.) George MacDonald, writing several generations ago, is undoubtedly right: "It may be infinitely less evil to murder a man than to refuse to forgive him. The former may be a moment of passion: the latter is the heart's choice. It is spiritual murder."

Contrast the pettiness of this poor Tennessee woman with the bigness of Abraham Lincoln. How often, when I am meditating on the subject of forgiveness, I think of this amazingly patient and merciful man. Lincoln selected the finest men he knew of to serve in his cabinet. He recognized their worth, although for the most part, fooled by his rustic manners and backwoods wit, they underestimated his. Secretary of State Chase, for instance, was a man of immense ability, all of which he quickly acknowledged. Chase chafed under his service to a man he considered his inferior. He kept his position for three years, often threatening to resign, sometimes actually doing so. Lincoln cajoled him into hanging on until, his patience having finally grown thin, he accepted one of Chase's notices. Not long after this incident, however a vacancy occurred in the Supreme Court and Lincoln appointed Chase its Chief Justice.

His counselors were astonished that Lincoln would appoint a man who had so often and so loudly scorned the President. There was no question to be resolved in Mr. Lincoln's mind, however. He simply considered Mr. Chase the best man for the job, so he forgave him any offense and put him back in high office. Our country has seldom seen such generosity. It was this same President, wasn't it, who taught us that when we make a friend of our enemy, we have destroyed our enemy? He had the wisdom to heed the advice of Solomon: "Do not pay attention to every word people say, or you may hear your servant cursing you" (Ecclesiastes 7:21). Lincoln refused to pay attention to what would cause him to think ill of others.

In high places of government and in humble places like home, there is no substitute for forgiveness. It frees us from the past, it loosens the grip of our own littleness, it makes for spiritual and emotional growth. A family cannot exist without it, friendships depend on it, and even our acquaintances rely upon it. Since we are surrounded by feeble human beings who will never rise to our level of expectation, we will either forgive or cut ourselves off from them.

What makes it so hard for us to forgive others, however is our disgust with ourselves. That means—

You Must Forgive Yourself

It isn't easy to accept ourselves, is it? I have a favorite incident that helps me keep myself in perspective on this matter. Throughout my ministry I have enjoyed short jokes. I am (that is, I used to be) the tallest member of my family and also of my wife's. Unfortunately, this younger generation, led by my own son, is passing me up. But being taller than my loved ones, I have not been terribly self-conscious about being five feet, six and a half inches high. My father, who never topped five four, boasted about the superiority of smallness. He said, "You look around. You see lots of little old men. You never see any big old men." He was convinced that we would live longer and live better because God had given us quality instead of quantity. I wholeheartedly agree.

But that hasn't kept me from having a lot of fun with short jokes. I have taken advantage of every one I have ever heard, and have received no little pleasure in abusing my tall friends. (They can't retaliate or they'd be guilty of picking on somebody who is not their size!) Anyway, on a Sunday morning a few years ago I was telling yet another short joke. The congregation loved it—all except one couple who stubbornly refused to crack a smile while everybody else was roaring with laughter—at least, it seemed to me they were roaring.

At the end of the service the couple met me at the door. They were disturbed. They didn't care if they never heard another short joke as long as they lived. With a tremble in her voice, the woman asked me, "When are you going to accept the fact that that's how God made you?"

I had something to say in retort, but I have to admit the woman was right on target. She thought I was calling attention to my diminutive stature because I was suffering feelings of inferiority. (Little did she know how we Lawsons pity big people!) She did not recognize my use of this "gimmick." (I come from a long line of important short gimmickers—George Gobel, Mickey Rooney, Napoleon Bonaparte). But she and I are in agreement—and in this we agree with the Scriptures—that spiritual well-being depends on accepting yourself as you are, as God made you. I must forgive myself for being short. You must forgive yourself for having certain characteristics that you do not like. What good will it do you to grow bitter about them, or try to hide them?

Remember my friends who suffered so deeply with their infant sons? They both said that what made their hurts so painful was that they not only had to deal with death or retardation, but with their almost crippling sense of guilt. If only they had done this, or had not done that, maybe the sons would have been all right. They could not keep from blaming themselves for the tragedies. Only later when they could open themselves to God's grace, were they able to forgive themselves and go on.

I'm not talking about cheap grace here. Some people stop their spiritual growth by forgiving themselves too easily. They major in forgiveness. My son says I do this to my body when we work at together at the health spa. "No pain, no gain," he keeps telling me, trying to force me to force my body to do more than it wants to. When it begins hurting, I forgive it. That, he tells me, will get me nowhere. The same laziness in spiritual dimensions gets the Christian nowhere also. We'll talk about this more in a later chapter.

What we must forgive is what God forgives—our mistaken values that we are exchanging for true ones, our moral lapses for which we are genuinely repentant, those botched relationships that we sincerely want to repair, our ignorance that we are studying to overcome. We must adopt the attitude of the scientist who has given ten years in his research only to discover that he has been pursuing a path that has led him to a dead end. He can bitterly denounce science in general and himself in particular for being so foolish, or he can quietly accept the fact that in science many research projects lead to dead ends, admit that he was wrong, and start again in another direction. Without forgiveness, he makes no progress. Neither do we.

Several years, before surgery for the condition was as common as it is now, a little girl was born with a cleft palate. In the thoughtless language of the day it was called a harelip. As she grew up she learned to shun people so they wouldn't make fun of her. Her resentment grew with her years. She became irritable; she hated the world and everything in it. She had no friends because she wouldn't let anybody get close enough to hurt her. Her sour attitude drove people away.

Then she underwent surgery. It went beautifully. She was a new woman, cured of her former deformity. At first she tried to adjust to her new appearance and tentatively reached out to other people. But she couldn't forget her past. Even though her appearance was normal now, she didn't really believe people would forgive her for her former self. She kept on alienating people. It was only when she received spiritual counseling that she was able to forgive herself for what she had been.

Christ has performed spiritual surgery on us. With divine scalpel He has removed our blemishes and transformed our characters. He has forgiven our sins and given us His Spirit to empower us to live like new beings.

But all He has done is without value unless we accept it. That means really believing we are forgiven. It means forgiving ourselves.

Without forgiveness, we cannot grow. Without forgiveness and forgiveness, and forgiveness. Unto seventy-seven times.

Discussion Starters for Small Groups

Think of the worst thing another person has ever done to you. What was it? Was it hard to forgive this person? What made it difficult?

Is it more difficult to forgive yourself or others? Why?

What does Matthew 18:21-35 teach us about why we should forgive others?

Where does a Christian's attitude of forgiveness come from?

CHAPTER THREE

"Please, Mother, I'd Rather Do It Myself"

1 John 1:1-7

I don't remember exactly, but I think it was an Anacin television commercial. An overly solicitous mother pushes her help on her daughter who is at the end of her tether. "Please, Mother I'd rather do it myself!"

Who wouldn't? Our drive toward independence probably starts in the terrible twos, if not earlier and it doesn't die until we do. Ironically, the more immature we are, the more we demand the right to do whatever we want to do in our own way. Maturity, however recognizes the impossibility of doing the most important things in life by ourselves. The things that really matter in life have to be done in cooperation with others.

As I was sitting in church last Sunday during our meditation period, I became aware of Dale Hillard beside me. He was presiding during our second service, as he regularly does. We tease each other a lot, so much so that our fellow members must wonder occasionally about our relationship. Last Sunday, however I had no doubt about the depth of my appreciation for and love of this man. We have served the Lord together and that mutual ministry has brought us very close in spite of the fact that we almost never have time to meet socially. If I were to try to do my ministry by myself, without Dale, I would be poorer. I have learned that I would rather not do it myself.

John writes that one purpose of preaching the gospel of Jesus Christ is *fellowship:* "We proclaim to you what we have seen and heard, so that you also may have fellowship with us. And our fellowship is with the Father and with his Son, Jesus Christ" (1 John 1:3). The cross of Christ represents God's supreme effort to bring us together with each other and with Him. God does not invite us to a solitary life of spirituality, but to a social life of genuine fellowship in Christ. You can't mature as a Christian by yourself.

Let me repeat: You can't grow up by yourself. As a newborn baby needs to be nurtured for years before he can claim adulthood, so a newly reborn Christian needs the help of his Christian family to assist him to maturity. That's why the writer of Hebrews says, "Let us consider how we may spur one another on toward love and good deeds. Let us not give up meeting together, as some are in the habit of doing, but let us encourage one another—and all the more as you see the Day approaching" (Hebrews 10:24, 25).

Somebody will object: "You don't have to belong to a church to be a Christian." It all depends on what kind of a Christian you want to be, mature or immature. I suppose you don't really have to raise a baby in a family, either. It depends upon what kind of a person you want the baby to grow up to be. Psychologists are pretty much agreed that one of the characteristics of a mature person is his capacity to form lasting and durable relationships. Spiritually immature persons break their relationships with people as soon as they no longer have any use for them. They cut off people who do things that don't please them. Over the years, then, they become increasingly isolated and, unfortunately, increasingly childish. They not only don't grow up, they grow down.

We Do Not Grow by Ourselves—We Heed Help

From the first day of the church, the earliest Christians helped each other. "They devoted themselves to the apostles' teaching and to the *fellowship,* to the breaking of bread and to prayer" (Acts 2:42). Why? Because they had just begun their Christian adventure; they wanted to know more, to enjoy more, to become more. They couldn't do it alone. Earlier when Jesus was starting His ministry, He gathered twelve men about himself so that He could teach them what they needed to know and, just as importantly, how to relate to one another.

The New Testament refers to the church as the family of God, the household of faith, the body of Christ. All these terms suggest a community of belief in which the members help each other.

Just a few weeks ago I read an article about Charles Colson, President Nixon's famous "hatchet man" who was convicted in the Watergate scandal. He received Christ shortly before his indictment. Asked how his conviction and prison experience affected his new faith in Christ, he said that for two years after his conversion everything went wrong. He was indicted, convicted, imprisoned; while he was in prison his father died and his teenage son was arrested on a drug charge.

What, then, sustained him during these dark days? Colson gives two answers: His knowledge that he had truly given himself to Christ, and the new Christian friends *who held on to him when everything was falling apart.* Colson freely admits that he needed help. Because of his friends he was able to survive and grow through his trials.

In the same issue of *Christianity Today*[1] there was an advertisement that caught my eye. It was for an organization called "Save the Children." Paul Newman and his wife, Joanne Woodward, were pictured with a caption that read, "We share our love with seven wonderful children we have never seen. We'd like to tell you why." The text explains that for sixteen years the actors have sent money to care for children. I was impressed that Colson's article and this advertisement were side by side, one testifying to the help he received, the other explaining the help Newman and Woodward were giving. This is fellowship: receiving **and** giving. Both are essential for growth.

We Need to Give Ourselves to Others

Dorothy Sayers has written, "If you insist on having your own way, you will get it. Hell is the enjoyment of your own way forever." This is pretty strong language, but very close to Scripture. Since Heaven is a pretty populated place, it won't be very attractive to those who can't bend themselves a bit for the sake of others. If they have to have their own way, Heaven's not for them. There is only one other possibility.

In my home church I learned the formula for joy: Jesus first, Others second, Yourself last. While it is not always as simple to apply as it sounds, it is still the best advice I have found for bringing Heaven to earth in one's life. All you have to do to experience Hell on earth is to turn it around and place yourself first, demanding that others serve you, giving you your way. You'll get what you want—and more.

When our daughter Kim was a three-year-old, she took over the kitchen one day. When her mother discovered what was happening, Kim pointed to her accomplishments. "I'm making a mess," she explained proudly. Not wanting to squelch her budding domestic talents, Joy pitched in to help her. All on her own, without having heard the television commercial, Kim stopped her. "Mama, I'd rather do it my selfish."

That's our natural tendency, all right—to do it ourselfish. It began with Adam and Eve. That's all they wanted, really—just to do it theirselfish. That's all Judas was after and he got paid thirty pieces of silver to boot. That's all the modern song preaches, isn't it? "And what's more, I did it my way."

But this propensity we have to do it ourselfish stands directly opposed to Jesus' teaching: "Love your neighbor as yourself." You can't do that and serve only yourselfish.

A baby begins life receiving. That's natural. When you bring a new baby home, everything in your house is affected. Schedules shift, furniture moves, meals change, sleep is altered for the sake of the baby. And nobody minds, because that's how it is with babies. But if the baby doesn't grow up after a while, everybody minds.

So in the spiritual realm it is fair to ask, How long will you demand that everything please you? Remember the purpose of the gospel fellowship? That means sharing, risking, giving ourselves to others.

It certainly does not mean being pleased all the time. Not long ago a woman gave me a catalog of things she didn't like about our church. She was so dissatisfied that she was going to leave us. As I read down the list of complaints, I was rather surprised to discover that most of the things she didn't like I don't like either. So why don't I leave with her? For one reason, because I have been to other churches and what I found there is the same as what I have found here: They have people in those churches, too. And whenever people get together you can count on it—they'll do some things I don't like.

There's another reason. What matters more than having the church please me in every particular is having genuine fellowship with other Christians, Christians who are often prickly, frequently hard to get along with, seldom jovial, occasionally very trying. In other words, like me. John pleads in his letter for us to understand that Jesus went to sacrificial lengths in order that we might have *fellowship,* sharing joys and sorrows, caring and sharing and crawling into the lives of just such imperfect but God-loved people.

You can do this only if you'll grow up.

You can grow up only if you do this.

Some members of the church I serve break my heart. They are deliberately stunting their growth. They won't serve, they won't give, they won't love. Then they wonder why they don't enjoy life the way other people seem to. They need fellowship.

We Need Fellowship with God

"And our fellowship is with the Father and with his Son, Jesus Christ. We write this to make our joy complete." John completes his triangle. Christian fellowship means sharing life with one another and with God.

I like what G. K. Chesterton has written:

Once I found a friend.
"Dear me," I said, "he was made for me."
But now I find more and more friends
Who seem to have been made for me
And more and yet more made for me.
Is it possible we were all made for each other all over the world?[2]

Of course it is. Being in fellowship with God is seeing with God's eyes, feeling with God's heart, crying godly tears, loving whom God loves. Fellowship with God calls us out of preoccupation with ourselves into involvement with others.

Alexander Solzhenitsyn, Russia's Nobel-Prize-winning author believes that "mankind's sole salvation lies in everyone making everything his business." What you are, then, is my business; what I am is yours. If I share with you both faith and love, then we make each other's welfare our common business. We express this fellowship when we commune together in the Lord. Think of the Lord's Supper: When we take of the cup and the bread, we draw close to Christ at His table and we draw close to our fellow participants.

This is why the "electronic church" can never really be a church. With whom are we communing? Martin E. Marty has satirically exposed this shallow substitute for worship. He notes that "Mr. and Mrs. Invisible Religion" get their kicks on Saturday night watching "born again" celebrities acting like "Holy Ghost entertainers" who are hosted by a charismatic entertainer in a highly professional but quite artificial program. On Sunday are Mr. and Mrs. Invisible Religion then going to make their way to a real church, with "offkey choirs, and sweaty and homely people who need them," people they really don't like and pastors who demand something of them?[4] They have found an easier substitute for the real thing.

Remember that advertisement with Paul Newman and Joanne Woodward? Something about it has been bothering me. "We share our love," they said, "with these children all around the world." No they don't. They send their money. Perhaps they do it in love, but what the children receive is food and clothing and shelter not love.

What would my children think if I said to them, "I want you to share my love. I'll send you a check once a month." They wouldn't call that love. Love is when you are there when they scrape their knees—or wreck your car—or flunk their exams—or announce their engagements. Love is being there when they make you proud and when they make you ashamed.

Let me tell you about a parent's love for his kids. I have even loved them when I didn't like them. The fact is, there have been some times when they've made me so angry I'd have to take a walk to cool off. Sometimes I have wanted to keep going. It hasn't always pleased me to be in fellowship with my children (and they have felt the same about me, they tell me). But if I had kept going, I would not have grown up. My children are, to a large extent, responsible for my maturity. They have forced me to behave, to sacrifice, to listen, even when I didn't want to. They have reminded me that the universe does not revolve around me. They have prevented my going through life me-first-ish, doing my own selfish.

That is precisely how the church works. In the family of God we are not all we ought to be. We are in fellowship. We don't give up on one another when displeased; instead, we help one another grow up.

Somebody added immeasurably to my theological understanding of the nature of the church by comparing mankind to a herd of porcupines at the North Pole. Think of your fellow Christians as porcupines in that arctic region. It is so cold there they are forced to huddle for heat, but when they get close, they stick and hurt each other so they draw apart. But then they get cold again, so they form another huddle—but that means more sticking and hurting, so they draw apart. And so on.

That's the nature of human relationships, even in the family of God. But painful as it is, these "porcupines" must keep huddling or they freeze. Or burn.

God's purpose is for us to have fellowship with one another—no matter how often we get stuck—and with Him. We enjoy fellowship with Him through our love for one another. John puts it this way:

Whoever does not love does not know God, because God is love. . . . If anyone says, 'I love God,' yet hates his brother he is a liar. For anyone who does not love his brother whom he has seen, cannot love God, whom he has not seen. And he has given us this command: Whoever loves God must also love his brother.

—1 John 4:8, 20, 21

So we band together in the church, on the whole a somewhat sorry lot, weaker than we ought to be, filled with deceit and cowardice and greed. A pretty prickly bunch. Yet when each sings with the others, "My faith looks up to thee," or "What a fellowship, what a joy divine, leaning on the everlasting arms," the Son and the Spirit and the Father with whom we fellowship became one with us and we grow into unity with God and with our brothers and sisters.

We grow together.

We can't do it ourselfish.

Discussion Starters for Small Groups

Do you agree or disagree with Dr. Lawson's statement that "the things that really matter in life have to be done in cooperation with others"? Give an example.

How do you react to Dorothy Sayers comment that "if you insist on having your own way, you will get it. Hell is the enjoyment of your own way forever"?

How is your fellowship with other believers related to your fellowship with God?

In the first two chapters of 1 John, what phrases are used to describe the experience of knowing God?

Are these phrases also descriptive of your fellowship with other believers? In what way?

How can you begin to make these phrases more descriptive of your relationship both with God and with others?

CHAPTER FOUR

"Father, I'd Rather Not Do It at All"

Galatians 6:1-10

I've been talking about spiritual growth as if this were a popular subject. I have assumed that whenever anyone is born again, he will automatically want to start growing up as a Christian. I know better of course. The truth is that many newborn believers like being spiritual babies. When God says, "My child, let me help you grow," many young Christians, of every age group, quickly answer Him, "Father I'd really rather not grow up. I want to stay where I am. Whatever You want me to do to become mature, I'd rather not do it at all."

They come in several varieties, these perpetual infants. Here are some of them:

The indulgers. They aren't bad people, you understand. It's just that when the alarm goes off on Sunday morning—if they even bothered to set it Saturday night—they roll over shut it off, and go back to their comfortable sleep. They have convinced themselves that it can't hurt them to miss worship. It'll get along without them and they can get along without it. They are Christians. Just ask them. But they aren't growing Christians. "Father I'd rather not do it at all."

The excusers. "I work six days a week, and Sunday is the only day I have to get any rest." "I used to work hard down at the church when the children were home, but now it's time for the younger people to take over. I deserve a rest." "I don't get anything out of church anyway. Why should I go? It does nothing for me." Etc., etc., etc. It all adds up to the same thing: "Father I'd rather not grow anymore."

The complainers. "All they want down at that church is my money. I'm sick and tired of it. I give what I intend to give and I'm not going to give a penny more." "They keep changing things down there. It's not like it used to be in the good old days." "As long as that old so-and-so is in charge, you can count me out." Same song, umpteenth verse: "Father I'd rather not grow anymore."

The withdrawers. "Nobody speaks to me at church. Nobody pays any attention to me." "I like to sneak in after the service has started and slip out during the benediction." "Church is okay, but I don't want to get involved." Just another variation on the theme, isn't it? "Father I'd rather not do it at all!"

Galatians 6:1-10 is just the prescription the doctor ordered for the idle. The apostle Paul leaves little room for taking it easy. Let's read it together:

Brothers, if someone is caught in a sin, you who are spiritual should restore him gently. *But watch yourself, or you also may be tempted. Carry each other's burdens* ["But Father I'd rather not"], and in this way you will fulfill the law of Christ. If anyone thinks he is something when he is nothing, he deceives himself. Each one should test his own actions. Then he can take pride in himself, without comparing himself to somebody else, *for each one should carry his own load.* ["But Father I'd rather not do my share at all!"].

Anyone who receives instruction in the word must share all good things with his instructor. [A Christian then can never be just a recipient of a preacher's or teacher's services; he must serve in return—even if he would rather not!]

Do not be deceived: God cannot be mocked. A man reaps what he sows. [Therefore if he sows nothing spiritually, he will reap the same.] The one who sows to please his sinful nature from that nature will reap destruction; the one who sows to please the Spirit, from the Spirit will reap eternal life. ["But Father I'd rather not sow at all!"] Let us not become weary in doing good, for at the proper time we will reap a harvest if we do not give up. Therefore, as we have opportunity, *let us do good to all people, especially to those who belong to the family of believers.* ["But Father I'd rather not do it at all!"]

The passage summarizes the elements of spiritual growth that we've studied so far. It takes for granted that the Christian will be a humble, forgiving partner in the body of Christ. It also adds a stern warning against the laziness and irresponsibility that prevent the desired maturation. We are never to grow weary in doing good, never to be unresponsive to the needs of any people, especially our fellow Christians, and never to think we can hoodwink God. If we do, we'll reap what we sow.

The Bible constantly reminds us that God is much more concerned about what we do than He is about what we promise. Jesus' parable of the two sons puts God's case as pointedly as possible:

"What do you think? There was a man who had two sons. He went to the first and said, 'Son, go and work today in the vineyard.'"

"I will not," he answered, but later he changed his mind and went.

"Then the father went to the other son and said the same thing. He answered, 'I will, sir,' but he did not go."

"Which of the two did what his father wanted?"

"The first," they answered.

Jesus said to them, "I tell you the truth, the tax collectors and the prostitutes are entering the kingdom of God ahead of you. For John came to you to show you the way of righteousness, and you did not believe him, but the tax collectors and the prostitutes did."

—Matthew 21:28-32

Why didn't the one brother obey his father after promising to do so? Was he rebellious? Did he hate his father? Probably not. Based on what we observe in ourselves, we can conclude he was just lazy or irresponsible.

What then shall we say of this brother's latter-day descendants?

Shall We Call Them Lazy or Irresponsible?

My poor children. How many sermons they have had to suffer on this subject at our house! I have such a fear that they may grow up to become like many adults I have tried to work with through the years, I'm afraid I've become a bit of a nag. I'm talking about basically good people, but undependable. They say they will do it, they promise to be there, they assure me I can count on them—but I end up picking up after them because they would rather not do it after all. I can't yell at them—they are supposed to be adults. So I preach to my kids instead. I use harsh words, words like duty and dependability and responsibility and trustworthiness and maturity. When I catch my children acting like these irresponsible or lazy adults, I ask them, "And how old are you?" I appeal to them to act their age, in the hope that when they are adults (as they really are becoming now) they will act as adults are supposed to.

My frustration with ungrown grownups is not unique to me, of course. Every leader of a group of people experiences it. Not long ago somebody left a copy of this lament on my desk. It has been around for many, many years. Do you recognize the four people? Do they go to your church?

Are You One of These People? This is a story about four people: Everybody, Somebody, Anybody, and Nobody. There was an important job to be done and Everybody was asked to do it. Everybody was sure Somebody would do it. Anybody could have done it, but Nobody did it. Somebody got angry about that because it was Everybody's job. Everybody thought Anybody could do it, but Nobody realized that Everybody wouldn't do it. It ended up that Everybody blamed Somebody when actually Nobody asked Anybody.

So, of course, it wasn't done. The rule of thumb in organizations is that no more than twenty percent of the members do at least eighty percent of the work and give eighty percent of the money. The rest would rather not be bothered.

This is not just a matter of organizational health, however. Personal maturity and mental health are involved. Psychiatrist M. Scott Peck writes in *The Road Less Traveled* that his chief enemy in his work to bring his patients to mental health is invariably their own laziness. He calls that laziness sin.

You wonder don't you, what they will think of themselves when in their old age, they review what they have accomplished in life. Ernest T. Campbell quotes Leonard Woolf, a prominent writer of a couple generations ago, who took such an inventory of his accomplishments and wrote himself off as a dismal failure. Finding that he had accomplished practically nothing, and that the world would have been as well off if he had played ping pong instead of attending committee meetings and writing books and memoranda, he made "a rather ignominious confession that I must have in a long life ground through between 150,000 and 200,000 hours of perfectly useless work."[1]

What a sad conclusion to reach when it is too late to do anything about those meaningless hours! It reminds one of Olmstead's Law: "After all is said and done . . . a lot more is said than done."[2] We say we want to do meaningful things—but we often say more than we are willing to do.

We feel it very important, though, to believe our work matters. This was the conclusion of a study conducted some time ago for a New England manufacturing firm. Among other questions, participants were asked, "Why do you work?" Surprisingly, the most frequent answer had nothing to do with money. "To feel useful," some said. "To have a sense of accomplishment," "To lead a productive life," they answered. People wanted to feel they counted for something to somebody. It was this unfulfilled longing that elicited Leonard Woolf's lament. Everybody would like to count for something—but then, not everybody would like to do what it takes to achieve this goal. The irresponsible or lazy person never gets there.

I am uncomfortably aware as I write these words that I belong among some of the chief offenders. In the church, people like me who have been Christians for a quarter of a century or more often begin to fade out of Christian activities or of genuine service to the Lord. We have grown tired or stale; we are stuck in our little routines. We have long since dedicated ourselves to schedules of sameness. In a word, we have stopped growing.

If it weren't for younger Christians whose enthusiasm makes up for their occasional lack of wisdom or judgment (qualities we old-timers pride ourselves on—to excuse our lack of enthusiasm), how would the Lord's work be done? While we devote uncounted hours to our important committee meetings and our frequent clusterings with fellow Christians, we rely on the youngsters in the faith to do the work of evangelism, and the work of service—in fact the work that God has called us to.

I'm afraid we may be as guilty as some Confederate veterans. After the decisive battle of Appomattox, an old farmer, loyal as he could be to the Confederate cause, decided to hire any of General Robert E. Lee's vets who needed a few days of work to make enough money to get

home. He was uneducated, but he was by no means ignorant.

He grouped the ex-soldiers into squads according to
their service rank. A visiting neighbor asked him about the
first group he saw. "Them is privates, sir, of Lee's army.
Very fine, sir: first-rate workers."

Then he asked about the second group. "Them is lieu-
tenants and captains, and they works fairly well, but not
as good as the privates."

When he asked about the third group, the colonels, and
what kind of workers they were, the wily old man answered, "Now, neighbor, you'll never hear me say one
word ag'in any man who fit in the Southern army; but I
ain't a-gwine to hire no generals."[3]

There really isn't much room for generals in the service
of the Lord, is there? Certainly not if the generals have
given up working in favor of ordering. We must not, Jesus
said, allow ourselves to become like the Gentiles who enjoy lording it over others; our leading is through serving—
and our growing comes through working (Matthew 20:25-
28).

Jesus hasn't called us to be the head of the church; He
reserved that role for himself. We've seen some many-
headed churches; they are monsters. A church needs only
one head, but it can use many hands and feet.

You may have already heard of the little French village
that boasted a lovely marble statue of Christ. During the
war, however, along with so much else in the village, the
statue was badly damaged. When peace came, the villagers lovingly collected the fragments and glued them
back together. But to their dismay, they couldn't find a
trace of the hands. Some of the villagers thought the
whole statue was ruined, since they couldn't imagine a
Christ without hands; but one of them had the imagina-
tion to transform the defect into a virtue. He attached a
plaque to the pedestal: "I have no hands but your hands."

Someone later penned these words, inspired by the in-
complete statue:

I have no hands but your hands to do my work today.
I have no feet but your feet to lead men on the way.
I have no tongue but your tongue to tell men how I died.
I have no help but your help to bring men to God's side.[4]

These words came back to me when Bob Wieland visited our church one Sunday morning. His testimony will never be forgotten by our congregation. The thirty-seven-year-old veteran of Viet Nam addressed us from his wheelchair. He had no legs to stand on; they were blown away in the war. He spoke to us about hunger and his determination to do something to relieve the world's starving population. We sat there in our well-fed comfort while he forced us to focus on the terrible toll hunger takes: twenty-eight people starving to death every minute, forty thousand a day, fourteen million a year.

Bob couldn't stand it. He had to do something. But what could a legless man do? He could use his arms, he decided. So on September 8, 1982 he left Knotts Berry Farm in California to begin his march for hunger across the United States, six million steps on his hands to Washington, D.C.

He could have said, "Father, I'd rather not! I have no legs. I am handicapped. Surely you don't expect me to do something like this?" He could have, but he didn't. So he uses what he has to serve the Lord. And he is growing!

Or Are They Growing?

I was thinking about Bob Wieland's courage at the same time the Philadelphia Phillies wrested their league championship away from the Chicago White Sox back in 1983. It was a painful series for me, since I really wanted the White Sox to take the series—but I also wanted the Phillies' Pete Rose to win.

I've been a Pete Rose fan since early in his Cincinnati Reds days. The more I learned about "Charlie Hustle," the more I liked him. According to an early scouting report, he should never have become the outstanding athlete he has been. "He can't run, he can't field, he can't hit from the left side and he can't make a double play," the scout said of Rose in the 1960's. "But he has a lot of hustle."

"That's how my dad taught me to play," Rose says. (He could have said, "But father, I'd rather not do it at all!") His advice to youngsters who want to play baseball? "Work hard. Work hard and have fun doing it. That's the easiest way to be successful." Of his father he said, "He always told me to give everything I had."[5]

Our Father says, "My child, give me everything you have. I'll help you grow into the person I intended you to be when I made you—and when I made you anew."

"But Father, I'd rather not do it at all."

William Wilberforce is one of England's giants, but you would have never known that to look at him. Small, sickly, and so unsightly that when he first stood before the British House of Commons, the members broke into embarrassed smiles. Then he began to speak and their smirks turned to respectful attention. This insignificant-appearing little man, more than any other person in England, over-turned his country's slavery institution. Giving everything he had to the cause of freedom for the slaves, he transformed himself into a giant along the way. Someone said of him, "The little minnow became a whale."

He could have said, "I'd rather not." He chose to grow.

No, there is no escape for us. The Scripture is too clear to argue away:

"Carry each other's burdens . . . fulfill the law of Christ."
"Each one should carry his own load."
"Anyone who receives instruction in the word must share all good things with his instructor."
"A man reaps what he sows."
"Let us not become weary in doing good."
"Let us do good to all people, especially to those who belong to the family of believers."

Even when we'd rather not do it at all!

Discussion Starters for Small Groups

React to the following statement: "I didn't mean to grow up spiritually. It just happened by accident."

Do you think this reflects the average Christian's expectation? experience? Explain your answer.

List as many "reasons" as you can that you have heard Christians give (or have given yourself) for their lack of spiritual growth.

What kinds of infants does Dr. Lawson list in this chapter? When have you recently acted like one of these?

What are some of the elements of spiritual growth summarized in Galatians 6:1-10?

What are some practical ways you can begin to implement these in your life this week?

What may keep you from doing so?

How may other believers help you overcome these hindrances to growth?

CHAPTER FIVE

Beware of Those Phony Detour Signs

Colossians 2:16-3:3

From the first halting silent movies to the latest technicolored, stereophonic-sound spectaculars, a favorite staple of our cinematic diet has been the chase scene. With the good guys hot in pursuit of the bad guys, or the bad guys on the heels of the good guys, or everybody after everybody else, the chase wakes up even the sleepiest audience.

One of the frequent ruses of the chase is the phony detour sign. It misdirects the pursuers, who rush madly into a lake or a blind alley or a dead end somewhere, while the prey escapes.

Phony detour signs are a lot older than the movies. People have been using them to their advantage for thousands of years. They are especially useful tools in controlling other people religiously. Even now a young Christian has to beware. In Colossians 2:16–3:3 the apostle Paul names four of them:

1. *Dietary Laws* (v. 16). "To be spiritual you must always

eat a certain food in a certain way on certain days, and never under any circumstances eat or drink what is forbidden!" In spite of the fact that Jesus declared all foods clean (Mark 7:19), even Christians can sometimes be bullied into measuring their "spirituality" by their diet. Scriptures like 1 Corinthians 8 and Romans 14 suggest that we may decide to restrict our diet for the sake of weaker Christians; that is the right motive. We are mistaken, however, if we think that dietary laws in themselves can help us grow in Christ.

2. *Proper observance of religious festivals or days* (v. 16). Should we celebrate the appearing of the new moon; and if so, how? Should we keep the Sabbath; and if so, how? Not too long after Paul wrote this letter, Christendom in fact was rent over the proper date for observing Christ's resurrection, so that today East and West claim different dates for Easter. A prominent religious sect refuses to celebrate Christmas because the precise date of Jesus' birth is not known. Its members have become sidetracked on an unimportant issue.

3. *Puffed-up self-promoters* (vv. 18, 19). Paul specifically mentions their "false humility" and "worship of angels." They boast of visions or special experiences with the Lord. While they protest that their much talking is to bring glory to God and not themselves, they cannot camouflage their inflated egos. They expect others to praise their superiority.

They are like the ship's captain who peered into the dark night and saw a faint light in the distance. He ordered his signalman to transmit a message: "Alter your course ten degrees south."

From the light in the distance came this prompt reply, "Alter your course ten degrees north."

Angry, the captain sent a second message: "Alter your course ten degrees south—I am the captain."

An immediate response signaled, "Alter your course ten degrees north—I am seaman third class Jones."

The captain would not be crossed. "Alter your course

ten degrees south—I am a battleship."

To which the not-so-distant light replied, "Alter your course ten degrees north—I am a lighthouse."[1]

All the captain's posturing could not change the truth: He was heading his ship into the rocks. Nor should any puffed-up self-promoter be allowed to detour us into spiritual disaster because he claims rank or special knowledge.

4. *The basic principles of this world* (vv. 20-23). "Human commands and teachings" do indeed often "have an appearance of wisdom," but their failure to restrain "sensual indulgence" gives them away. Of these principles the prophet Isaiah exclaims in the name of the Lord, "The wisdom of the wise will perish, the intelligence of the intelligent will vanish" (29:14).

With so many detour signs along a Christian's road to maturity, what's the new believer to do? How can he wend his way through the thicket of conflicting signals?

He can remember four rules of the road: (1) Refuse to let anyone judge you but Christ. (2) Keep close to Christ, close enough to see where He is going. (3) Remain connected to the Head as a part of the whole body. (4) Give yourself only to what won't perish. We'll examine each rule.

Refuse to Let Anyone Judge You but Christ
Colossians 2:16

Paul writes, "Therefore do not let anyone judge you...." We must pay attention to what precedes his therefore. He builds a pretty solid case for Christ's right to judge—and no one else's:

- You received Christ as your Lord (6).
- You now live in Him (6).
- You must not allow yourself to become captivated by "hollow and deceptive philosophy, which depends on human tradition and the basic principles of this world" (8).
- Christ is head over every power and authority (10).
- You were baptized into Christ and raised with Him from the dead (12).

• God made you alive with Christ and forgave your sins (13).

In view of all these, then, you must not let anyone judge you according to any of this world's standards. Do not be fooled. It certainly is easier to follow prescriptions about festivals or rituals or special holy days than to live in Christ. If we can only do some remarkable work to attract God's attention, or perform some prescribed ritual, or give Him honor during a declared holy day ("Yes, I always worship on Christmas and Easter"), others can measure our Christianity and render judgment on our so-called spirituality.

This was a leading motive in the medieval cult of discomfort among monks and hermits. These men devoted themselves to attracting attention by performing superhuman feats of self-denial. A Cilician monk called Conon lived for thirty years on one meal a week. Another named Adolus restricted himself to three hours of sleep a night; another one, Sosoes, spent his nights on a jutting crag so that if he dozed off he would fall to his death. Pachomius denied himself the comfort of lying down to sleep; he stood in his cell instead.[2] These theatrics could be matched by thousands more. In spite of the enormous commitment with which these men pursued spirituality, we give them our pity rather than our praise, for they sped down a detour to nowhere. Such meaningless stunts are the very opposite of Christ's will for His followers.

A book was published in 1979 with the title, *Free to Act: How to Star in Your Own Life*, I have not read the book and don't intend to but the title stopped me dead. Here's the hermits' problem: They think the Christian life is a performance in which they have been cast as stars. If they act well their part, the audience (God, fellow believers, the whole world) applauds. Nobody else is helped by it, the world is not enriched by it, but they do get good at it.

One thing is certain: When we busy ourselves about improving our own act, we'll lose sight of Christ, who keeps moving on ahead of us. One old man had claimed to be a disciple of Jesus. He loved to boast that he had never been in a tavern, that no alcoholic drink had ever touched his lips. In addition, he had never smoked tobacco and he had never been to a house of prostitution. Then he would wait, after reciting these virtues, for the applause. He was like a latter-day monk, forcing his body into submission in the guise of discipleship. In reality, he was just starring in his own performance.

By the way, the good gentleman never included in his inventory that he had along the way acquired a reputation for shady business practices, that he was a slum landlord, that he had gone through four wives, and that he had neglected to add to his virtues humility.[3]

Keep Close to Christ, Close Enough to See Where He Goes
Colossians 2:17

Jesus doesn't stop to admire our flawless performance on our self-chosen stage, He keeps pressing ahead to people who need Him and can be helped by His followers. Wise, then, is the Christian who follows the Lord and remains uncommitted to anything or anyone else. When our lives are centered on Him, we'll fret less over the hundreds of minor matters that have splintered Christianity. We'll stop trying to attract everyone's attention to our brand of spiritual achievement and instead promote *Him*.

Focus on Jesus. There is an old story of Leonardo da Vinci and his masterpiece, "The Last Supper." He had apparently invested great pains to present a wealth of detail on the two cups standing on the table. When a friend viewed the unfinished painting, he stared with wondrous appreciation at these cups. Da Vinci saw his reaction and seized a paintbrush and with a sweep of his hand he painted the cups out of the picture. "Not that," he told his friend, "that isn't what I want you to see! It's the face. Look at the face!"

Christians must also keep looking at the face of the Lord and not at the instruments of worship. It is possible, we confess ruefully, to become so occupied in the noble task of spreading Christianity that we have no time to think of Jesus. We serve on committees and plan our programs and sing in our choirs and build our buildings and dispatch our missionaries—just as we would faithfully do our jobs down at the plant or office. We're good workers; we'll do our jobs, even if we forget Him for whom we are doing them. In our busy-ness we can easily be led astray by a phony detour sign.

Stay Connected to the Head (As a Part of the Body)
Colossians 2:19

Paul refers to the body of Christ, which "grows as God causes it to grow." The God who designed the flowers that grow and bloom according to His plan also designed the church that depends on the Lord for its growth. Puffed-up self-promoters make themselves sound indispensable to God and the church, but the Bible presents Jesus as the one irreplaceable Head of the church. If the church and any individual member of the body are to grow, it will be through their connection with the Head.

And the Head defines growth in terms of service, not star performances or adherence to rituals. "Christ is passing out no kingships now, only crosses. Christ teaches us how to give more, not how to get more; how to suffer, not how to escape; the importance of sharing, not the necessity of hoarding; how to be a servant, not how to demand special privilege; how to handle a towel, not a scepter."[4]

Staying connected with Jesus, then, means that His disposition rules us, His orders control us, His love compels us. We are prepared to serve Him at any cost, no matter where or under what conditions until He rescinds His orders.

Ours will be the loyal obedience of Lieutenant Hiroo Onoda of the Japanese Imperial Army. When he arrived on the remote Philippine island of Lubang in 1944, his commanding officers gave him his orders: "To continue carrying out your mission even after the Japanese army surrenders, no matter what happens." That was in 1944.

In March 1974 a record crowd jammed into Tokyo International Airport to greet Lieutenant Onoda, the last Japanese holdout of World War II. He had just surrendered, more than twenty-eight years after the official end of the war.

When his island was liberated by American and Philippine forces in 1945, Onoda and three other enlisted men went underground. One of them surrendered in 1950; another was killed in a shootout with Philippine police in 1954, and the third of them in 1972. Onoda kept serving.

He was finally persuaded to surrender in 1974 when his terms were met: "Only in case my commanding officer rescinds my order in person will I surrender." His officer was located in Kyushu, where he worked as a bookseller; he was flown to the Philippines, where he read out the Imperial Army order of September 1945: "As of this moment, all officers and men under this command shall terminate all hostilities."

Onoda laid down his gun.

Did he feel, after all these years, that his obedience had been in vain? No, he said, "when my purpose in war has been attained, in the fact that Japan today is rich and great, to have won or lost the war is entirely beside the point."[5]

He stayed close to his commander. He obeyed his orders. He rejoiced that his country prospered. He accepted the temporary military defeat of his country because something better had taken place. What mattered to him more than anything else was his country's prosperity.

What matters more than anything else to you? You have to be able to answer this question to keep yourself from being easily detoured.

Give Yourself to What Won't Perish
Colossians 2:20−3:3

Don't let this world's principles tighten their grip on you. They are destined to perish. You aren't. "Since, then, you have been raised with Christ, set your hearts on things above." Give yourself to the real thing.

I have kept a Christmas card for years because I treasure the sender and the message. A young artist who gave me the privilege of baptizing him into Christ further honored me the following Christmas by hand-lettering the following poem. We don't know who wrote it, but whoever did captured the Christian's desire to set his heart and mind on things above:

Not I but Christ be honored, loved, exalted.
Not I but Christ be seen, be known, be heard,
Not I but Christ in every look and action,
Not I but Christ in every thought and word.

Such devotion is not natural, of course. In a world as attractive as ours, it requires courage to be so committed; but it is thus that we Christians commit ourselves to Jesus Christ. Our objective is to think about Him, imitate Him, honor Him, and in every other way center our lives on Him. We do all this for partly selfish reasons: we don't want to devote our lives to only what this world offers. Its rewards aren't good enough. We want something better.

I have enjoyed following the career of Bjorn Borg, the masterful tennis pro who announced his retirement in February, 1983. The only man ever to win six French opens and the first to claim five consecutive Wimbledon championships since Laurie Doherty in 1906, Borg epitomizes the best in tennis to many of his fans, including me. Since the ninth grade this committed athlete practiced his skill at least four hours a day. (His trainer said he would know when Borg was finished—it would be when he would take a shortcut and train for only two hours a day.)

When he retired, one reporter wrote that his athletic skill had not run down, but "his ability to concentrate" had. He had married; his discipline was damaged by his contentment. As far as he was concerned, he had found something better than the accolades of the professional tennis circuit. He had found love.[6] It lasts.

You have given yourself to new life in Christ; you have died to the temporary pleasures of this deceiving world. Jesus, who is your Savior, has also become your model. Don't be fooled, then, by any phony detour signs. Remain close to Jesus, close enough to follow Him and Him alone. He'll lead you to life everlasting. Only He is Lord of the life that lasts.

Discussion Starters for Small Groups

What are the spiritual detours listed in Colossians 2:16—3:3?

How does each of these detours sidetrack you from growing spiritually?

Describe a time in your Christian life when you were caught up in external rules and regulations. What were they? How did it happen? How did you redirect your focus?

Do you feel that you are giving more time and attention to Christ or the church? Is there a difference?

Why does it seem to be so much easier to focus on external things or man-made rules than on a vital relationship with Christ?

CHAPTER SIX

"Don't Sweat the Small Stuff"

Matthew 6:25-34

When I received the word that my stepfather was in a coma, I knew that death could not be far away. At eighty-seven, he had pushed well past his three score years and ten, and his health had been failing for the past few years. The end of consciousness was a signal that the time had come for us to get ready for the end of his earthly life.

Joy and I grabbed a flight to Oregon in order to be with him—and my mother, who was ten years younger but not able to be by herself. In the lingering days that followed, we put in long hours as we visited in the hospital, arranged a legal guardianship for Mother, sorted and scrubbed and disposed of the mobile home and its contents, sought and found a good nursing home for Mother while also seeking more permanent care for Jack if he should survive his stroke, then arranged for and conducted his funeral when he died after nearly two weeks in his coma.

Busy, difficult days. The strain showed one day in

the attorney's office. After conducting my business, I left, only to return immediately to seek some important papers, which the secretary assured me she did not have, and which I then found in my jacket pocket. I blushed. She scolded. "Just cool it," she said, "Just cool it."

I tried to, but it isn't easy to be cool under stress. Cardiologist Robert Eliot prescribes two rules for minimizing tension: "Rule number 1 is, don't sweat the small stuff. Rule number 2 is, it's all small stuff. And if you can't fight and you can't flee, flow."[1]

It is pretty good advice. I've given it myself to people like me trying to cope with death and dying, or with marriage and family difficulties. I've even counseled conscientious Christians, uptight about their spiritual development, not to sweat the small stuff. They were trying too hard, worrying too much about pleasing God. Even though they believed that Christians are saved by grace, they were fretting lest they weren't working hard enough to insure their salvation. These sanctified worrywarts need to be reminded that Jesus' yoke is easy and His burden light (Matthew 11:30). He gives rest for the soul, even in the most trying circumstances.

What the attorney's secretary didn't know was that throughout our two weeks of frenetic activity, Joy and I were experiencing peace. We weren't "sweating the small stuff." We were being frequently surprised as God seemed to be walking ahead of us, dissolving problems that we couldn't see any way around, and surrounding us with a sense of His presence.

Through those days my mind returned again and again to Matthew 6:25-34. "Therefore I tell you, do not worry about your life. . . ." We did not worry. We trusted that everything we needed would be given us. And it was, as it has always been for us. God keeps His promises.

Jesus urges us to make strength of mind our goal. There is a difference between the "peace of mind" that many misguided people aim for and the tough faith that Jesus preaches. "Each day has enough trouble of its own" is not the saying of a blind optimist who believes that if you just believe, then everything you believe will come true. No, you can't believe death away from a tired old man even though his wife still needs him to take care of her. Nor can you believe away her failing memory and stiff joints. We knew, as we took over their affairs, that our future would be filled with the troubles we were now assuming and no amount of "believing" would change that fact. But strength of mind and trust in God could keep us from "sweating the small stuff."

Don't Sweat Your Physical Well-Being

"Do not worry about your life, what you will eat or drink; or about your body, what you will wear." You probably remember that old tale of the rich Oriental ruler who couldn't shake himself out of his discontentment. In desperation he appealed to a famous wise man to help him find peace of mind. The sage told him to seek out the most contented man in his kingdom and wear his shirt. The ruler dispatched his couriers into the four corners of his realm. One of them found a man who was thoroughly contented, and brought him to meet the ruler. The problem was, the man had no shirt.

Shirts and food and drink and additional hours to live are not worth worrying about, Jesus insists, since God has accepted responsibility for these provisions. He has other things in mind for us to be concerned with.

Like the kingdom of God. The Lord has not changed His mind. Clear back in the Ten Commandments He told His people that they were to have no other gods before Him (Exodus 20). They were not to be idolators, allowing some other god to take His place in their priorities. If they would keep Him first, He would take care of their physical needs.

That was the source of our confidence during my stepfather's last illness. We knew God would take care of him, even through death. Since He is Lord of the living and the dead, and since He has promised life beyond death to those who are His (1 Corinthians 15 and John 11), we

really had nothing to worry about. Anyway, all our worrying could not add another hour to his life. There is a sense
in which, as we stand before the immensity of eternity,
even life itself on this planet is "small stuff," not to be
worried about. Only the kingdom of God—that is, the rule
of God in our lives—deserves such attention.

This is admittedly a difficult lesson for Americans to
learn. We equate busy-ness with success. We scorn inactiv-
ity as sloth and misinterpret trust as foolhardiness. We
would not know how to take Robert Louis Stevenson's
criticism of the super-busy people of his century—before
things speeded up! "Extreme busyness," he wrote,
"whether at school, kirk (church) or market, is a symptom
of deficient vitality." Deficient vitality? Didn't he mean
"abundant" or "unusual" vitality? No, he meant what he
said, adding that such people have a nature that "is not
generous enough" to allow them to be idle. The result is
that they hurry through life, busy about this and that,
worrying about every detail, so that they arrive at the end
of their days without ever having really lived any of them.
It takes quiet to grow; it requires rest from labor, moments
for meditation, generous pauses for prayer.

That is why, when you are trying so hard to grow as a
Christian, sometimes the best advice you can be given is
not to try so hard. Just as your fretting can't add any days
to your life, neither can your striving for perfection make
you perfectly spiritual. Strive for one thing: trust in the
Lord, who makes your striving unnecessary.

Don't Sweat Your Future Well-Being

"Therefore do not worry about tomorrow, for tomorrow
will worry about itself." Living by faith today acts as a
preventive against disaster tomorrow. Living in fear today
practically guarantees that the trouble you fear tomorrow
will occur. You have willed it! One of the "inexorable laws"
of fear according to Dr. Paul Tournier, is that "fear creates
what it fears." He mentions the beginning skier whose fear
of falling makes him fall; the fearful lover who holds back

because he's afraid he'll lose his loved one—so he does.[2]
Is it possible to live today without undue concern for tomorrow? Jesus says so.

When we were tending to the multitudinous details concerning my stepfather's dying and death and my mother's
pressing needs, we had to make several plans. If Jack
should live, we must do A. If he dies, we must do B and C.
If Medicare covers the costs, then we'll do D. If not, we
must adopt plan E. If all six of the children agree, then we
can proceed with F. If not, then G must be put into effect.
What shall we do with the car, the mobile home, the personal effects? More difficult, what can we do for the very
sick dog who is so deeply loved by both Mother and Jack?
To put him to sleep will break their hearts; to let him live
invites additional disease and unsanitary living conditions. Where should Mother live, and how?

So many decisions, so little wisdom. Yet each day my
mind returned to Jesus' words. "Do not worry about tomorrow." Each day, then, we dealt with the decisions that
day forced on us; each day we also made plans for tomorrow, but we constantly reminded ourselves that they were
tentative plans, ones that we could alter or scrap in an
instant if necessary. We did not dare let our wisdom get in
God's way. He was intent on blessing us and meeting our
needs even in the midst of our sorrow. We would get
ready for tomorrow, but we would not worry about it.
When tomorrow would come God would be there.

We tried to adopt the stance of Abraham Lincoln. Early
in his political career he impressed his contemporaries by
his apparent tranquility regarding the outcome of his races
for office, many of which he lost. For example, he made
this speech in New Salem:

> Gentlemen and fellow citizens: I presume you all know
> who I am. I am humble Abraham Lincoln. I have been
> solicited by many friends to become a candidate for the
> legislature. My politics are short and sweet, like the old
> woman's dance. I am in favor of a national bank. I am

in favor of the internal improvements system and a high protective tariff. These are my sentiments and political principles. If elected, I shall be thankful; if not, it will be all the same.

In the words of Dr. Eliot, Lincoln was not sweating the small stuff. He was not fretting over his future well-being. He exhibited here the calm he maintained, even with his heart breaking in the stress of his wartime presidency. He made tentative plans for the future, of course, but he let each day's trouble be sufficient for itself. Just a few verses later in the Sermon on the Mount, Jesus explains why we can enjoy a sense of well-being even in the face of tomorrow's uncertainties.

Ask, and it will be given to you; seek, and you will find; knock, and the door will be opened to you. For everyone who asks receives, he who seeks finds, and to him who knocks, the door will be opened.
—Matthew 7:7, 8

At first reading these verses seem too good to be true. He'll give me anything I want? Even that new Porsche 928? Or the lakeside summer home I've been dreaming about? Or grandchildren? Anything?

I'm not sure about the Porsche, I'll admit. What Jesus said earlier is, "Seek first his kingdom and his righteousness, and all these things (food, drink, clothing) will be given to you as well." The promise is for all the necessities and more. The truth is that anyone who adopts God's sense of values finds his shopping list of wants strangely altered. Advertisements have less appeal, trends less attraction, fads and fashions less allure. He really wants God's rule in his life and on his planet.

George MacDonald has correctly identified the reason we don't more readily get what we want by seeking God's righteousness. We have lesser things in mind. "Man finds it hard to get what he wants, because he does not want the best; God finds it hard to give, because He would give the best, and man will not take it."[3]

My weeks in my hometown tending to family matters made me aware once again of how many times God has given me the best, even when it looked for a while as if He had turned His back. In everything He has worked "for the good of those who love him who have been called according to his purpose" (Romans 8:28). My family has had its share of heartbreaks. In my teen years my parents were divorced. About the same time my father lost his business and was reduced to poverty. Both my sister and my brother have suffered through divorce. Ill health and death are not strangers to us. Yet my testimony is really praise, not complaint. God has used every reversal in my life to the good of my ministry. Every apparent defeat He has turned into later victory.

He has proved that I have nothing to fear tomorrow.

I don't have to worry about future well-being.

Don't Sweat Your Past, Either

Meditating on these verses in my hometown gave me an added perspective. Jesus doesn't mention the past here, but as I took to heart His counsel about tomorrow, I realized that I could trust in God's providence in the future because of what He has done for me in the past.

The past was often before me during these days. Mine is a small town, still populated with people who have been important to me for many years. Good friends—with long memories. They love to recall this or that incident from my childhood and youth. Every time I go home the stories seem to have grown a little more. They tease me. This time, though, I got even.

I reminded them that even if everything they say about my wicked, wicked past is correct, it doesn't make any difference because of something they taught me in that wonderful home church of mine. During my morning sermon I pointed to the baptistry and told them that whatever they say about my past is irrelevant. More than that, it's forgotten. My Christian brothers and sisters led me to that baptistry years ago, where as a believer in the grace of the Lord Jesus Christ I entered the waters of baptism and buried my past. Baptism is God's promise of forgiveness of sins, His assurance of resurrection into a new life in Christ (see Romans 6). So no Christian has to worry about his past. It's dead and God has forgotten it.

Christians don't have to worry about their past being found out. They do not lead hidden lives. Having had their sins forgiven, they can live without fear of disclosure. They then seek God's righteousness, living honestly before Him and everyone else, having nothing to conceal. Zest for living replaces guilt; enthusiasm returns. Being in Christ washes away secrets and secretiveness as surely as baptism into Christ cleanses the repentant sinner of his guilt before God.

So don't sweat your past.

Instead, Live for the Lord Today

"Seek first his kingdom and his righteousness"—today. Look for the good that God is doing for you through today's circumstances.

When Dietrich Bonhoeffer was jailed by the Nazis, he could not imagine what good his incarceration was doing. He did not want his outside correspondents to think him disgruntled, however because he wasn't. "Much as I long to be out of here," he wrote, "I don't believe a single day has been wasted. What will come out of my time here it's still too early to say; but something will come of it."[4] What did not come was Bonhoeffer's release. He died shortly before the end of the war. A skeptic could scoff at Bonhoeffer's "groundless" optimism, but the skeptic would be wrong. Never did the young theologian presume to demand that God effect his release. Nor did he limit the good to come from his imprisonment to something he very much desired, his freedom and continued life. What he expected was that his imprisonment would not be wasted.

It wasn't. God has used it and Bonhoeffer's writings in prison to bring hope and new insight to millions of believers. Bonhoeffer sought the kingdom of God. God gave him that and more—a powerful influence upon later generations of Christians. The prisoner's faith in God was not a prescription for release, but a steadying source of strength in a most difficult situation—strength for him and for others.

Our struggles to care for my dying stepfather and widowed mother do not compare with Bonhoeffer's days of Nazi horror but we experienced the peace that blesses those who live one day at a time for the Lord, trusting Him to bring good out of grief. He gave us everything we needed and more. We meditated on the words of Psalm 37:

> Trust in the Lord and do good;
>   dwell in the land and enjoy safe pasture.
> Delight yourself in the Lord
>   and he will give you the desires of your heart.
> Commit your way to the Lord;
>   trust in him and he will do this:
> He will make your righteousness shine like the dawn,
>   the justice of your cause like the noonday sun.
> Be still before the Lord and wait patiently for him.

I have written quite personally in this chapter—not offensively so, I hope—in order to add a word of praise to my words of instruction in spiritual growth. Throughout this book we have been exploring the ingredients of Christian growth and development. I haven't offered any list of ten easy steps to instant spirituality. Instead, I have tried to look at a few Scriptures that I have found helpful in my own growth. This one has been especially helpful, but may not seem very helpful to the young Christian. You want to be up and doing for God! You are eager to prove yourself worthy of your new name. That's commendable, and I congratulate you on your enthusiasm.

Don't let me dampen it in any way. I'm just looking ahead a bit. Eagerness so quickly leads to a desire to be perfect, and perfectionism leads just as quickly to discouragement, and discouragement expresses itself often in worry. That's why this passage is so important—don't worry. Don't worry about food and drink and clothes. Don't worry about life, how many days yours will have. Don't worry about anything. Just keep the Lord as your top priority, and let Him take care of you. You'll grow in Him as surely as the young sapling grows into a strong tree.

Several years ago, when aviation was very young, a French pilot named Antoine de Saint-Exupery found himself socked into the middle of a dense fog somewhere beyond his point of departure but far short of his destination. Today's sophisticated electronic assistance was not available then, and the pilot was already shrugging his shoulders in resigned helplessness. He was down to an hour of fuel, much less than he needed to reach Cisneros, even if he could see to get there. Radio beams were reaching him, so he knew approximately where he was, but no landing strip was within his fuel time.

One by one he received radio messages from somewhere out there in the fog. Agadir, Casablanca, Dakar. They couldn't do anything to help, but they sent words of encouragement to Saint-Exupery. But such words would not save his life if he had to make a crash landing in the fog.

Then suddenly, without a word of greeting, from three thousands miles away, Toulouse burst through. Toulouse, the headquarters of Saint-Exupery's line. They knew him in Toulouse, they knew his plane, they were responsible for this assignment. Without a word of greeting, Toulouse went straight to the point: "Your reserve tank's bigger than standard. You have two hours of fuel left. Proceed to Cisneros."[5]

They couldn't rescue him from his plight, but they could make it possible for him to get out of it. They did nothing, really, but overcome his despair by assuring him that he carried more fuel than he supposed. His reserve tank would see him through. It was larger than standard.

So is ours.

And why do you worry? . . . For the pagans run after all these things, and your heavenly Father knows that you need them. But seek first his kingdom and his righteousness, and all these things will be given to you as well.

                              —Matthew 6:28, 32, 33

Discussion Starters for Small Groups

List several things you are worried about right now.

Why do these things cause you to worry?

What would God have to do to alleviate these worries?

Why do you think seeking the kingdom of God helps you overcome worry?

What can you do to replace worry with trust?

How can you help others to do the same?

CHAPTER SEVEN

A Special Grace That God Gives

2 Corinthians 8:1-9

If I were Secretary of the Treasury in the Lord's administration, I would exempt two classes of people from paying tithes and giving offerings to His work. Poor widows, on limited income and with no hope of increasing their revenue, should not be expected to give anything; they need everything they can get. Such would be my reasoning.

I would come to the same conclusion about poor families, especially families with children. They need help, not more expenses.

The Lord, however, doesn't agree with me. In fact, it was a widow that Jesus singled out for commendation because she not only tithed but gave everything—"all she had to live on" (Mark 12:41-44). Rather than commenting on her foolishness in not saving the little she had, Jesus held her up as an example.

In 2 Corinthians 8 the apostle Paul speaks glowingly of some poor families in Macedonia (Northern Greece) who, in spite of their extreme poverty, pleaded for the privilege of giving money to help destitute Christians in Jerusalem, people who were only slightly worse off than the Macedonians themselves. And when the standard of living of these people in Thessalonica, Philippi, and Berea is compared with ours, they seem to be barely hanging on to the bottom rung of the poverty ladder. Yet when they heard of someone else in need, they quickly offered the little they had.

I wouldn't make a very good Secretary of the Treasury for the Lord, would I? I'm afraid I'm too money-conscious for His kingdom.

You may be like me. If so, you and I need to study God's economics very carefully, because if we don't grow up in our management of our money, we won't grow up!

Look carefully at what the Bible says about these Macedonian Christians: "Out of the most severe trial [They were persecuted for their faith and impoverished in their finances.] their overflowing joy [Can poor people be joyful?] and their extreme poverty welled up in rich generosity" (2 Corinthians 8:2).

The Macedonian Christians give us a new definition of wealth don't they? They had few material possessions, but they were joyful and generous—rich, Paul says, in generosity. This is finally the only true measure of wealth, isn't it? It isn't how much money you have, but how generous you are with what you have, that marks you as a wealthy person. The generous are the only truly rich.

John Steinbeck, the famous novelist, tells of his friend's uncle, a very rich millionaire, who experienced financial reversal during the great depression. In a few short weeks his assets dropped from seven million to two million. That's two million dollars in cash. He became very depressed, complained that he didn't know how he would even be able to eat, limited his breakfast to one egg and the other meals so severely that he began to look gaunt and haggard. In the end he shot himself. He didn't want to statue.

Impoverished, yet he had two million dollars.

John Jacob Astor IV gave us this unforgettable insight into riches in the 1890s (to my knowledge, he was not known to make any other immortal remarks): "A man who has a million dollars is as well off as if he were rich." When Astor went down with the Titanic he left behind eighty-seven million. Obviously, by the dollar standard, he was a rich man. But what kind of a standard is the dollar if a man with two million of them commits suicide out of fear of starvation?

Wealth has to be defined as something other than the accumulation of bunches of bucks. Somewhere in the definition must be the word *generosity*. And generosity, according to the apostle Paul, derives from the grace of God rather than the greatness of the assets.

An Example of That Grace
2 Corinthians 8:1-5

The Macedonian Christians gave all they could and more. Paul seems surprised by the size of their contribution. Like me, he might have been hesitant to ask such poor people to help relieve the suffering of the Jerusalem Christians, unless, also like me, he had found the poor more eager to share their little than the rich were to share their much. How could these Christians do this? Paul has a simple explanation.

First, *they gave themselves to the Lord.* Nobody had to tell them that giving is proof of devotion. You can protest your love for someone all you want, but it is only in your giving that you prove you mean what you say. These Christians loved the Lord, loved Him enough to give whatever they could—and more—for His people's needs.

Giving proves your love. During World War II a draft board director used this principle to sniff out phony conscientious objectors who were trying to escape the draft on the grounds that their religion prohibited their bearing arms. His method was simple. He asked each alleged objector for the name of his church. Then he solicited from the church the financial record. He wanted to know whether the man tithed, because the director was convinced that if a man didn't have enough faith to be a tither, he certainly didn't have enough faith to be a conscientious objector.

Nothing proves your love or your faith like your giving. Some people claim that it's hard to tithe. It probably is, if you are giving only because the preacher tells you to, or because your church budget needs more money, or because of a new building drive. But if you love the Lord and believe His promises, generosity in your support of the Lord's kingdom is as easy as can be.

My son recently gave me a good illustration of this principle. It was his high-school homecoming weekend, and he had a date with his steady girlfriend. To this antiquated parent, Lane seemed to be squandering an enormous amount of money on the event new clothes, flowers, dinner. When I snorted my disapproval, he didn't seem the least bit penitent. All he said was, "She's worth it."

So she is. I'm afraid my son is smitten. The proof is in his readiness to spend his hard-earned money on her. (And when you are a restaurant dishwasher—even the head dishwasher, as he is, the money is hard-earned indeed.) If he refused to be a little extravagant, I'd doubt his sincerity. So would she.

The more I study about the cults like Jimmie Jones' People's Temple and others, the more impressed I am with the high level of giving that is expected of their members. Jones' followers regularly contributed twenty-five percent or more of their earnings. There can be no question of their devotion, debate as we may about their motives. Having given themselves to Jones, they were ready to give their money.

"Then," Paul adds, they gave themselves "to us in keeping with God's will." They jumped aboard his ministry, because he was serving their Lord. They supported him, contributed to the cause for which he was raising money; they prayed for him, sustained him through his darkest hours, and in every way became one with him.

Encouragement to Enjoy the Same Grace
2 Corinthians 8:6-9

From the Macedonian Christians Paul turns his attention to his friends in Corinth, where the economy is much more robust and the Christians enjoy a higher standard of living. Surely they will want to do as much as the Macedonians are doing. Paul's colleague Titus will soon be coming to Corinth to receive their offering for Jerusalem. They have already started collecting it; now Paul urges them to complete "this act of grace on your part."

Time after time Paul mentions grace in chapters 8 and 9. It is a word refulgent with meaning. It often suggests God's merciful treatment of undeserving sinners like us, but here it shows another of its many sides. The "act of grace" here is an offering. Not just any offering, but a giving up of hard-earned and somewhat scarce money for a cause dear to the Lord's heart, so dear that He enables the donor to offer what he otherwise would not be able to give up. There is a touch of the divine in this generosity.

Furthermore, this generosity is essential to maturity. Paul makes an impressive list of the accomplishments of these Corinthian Christians: They excel "in faith, in speech, in knowledge, in complete earnestness and grace of giving." Little giving, little growing.

If they are to follow the Macedonian example, they too must first give themselves to the Lord. When they do, they also will quickly prove their love and enjoy the help of God in their giving—and in everything else.

This is what happened to Warren Moore of Portland, Oregon. In 1962 his church printed his tithing testimony in its weekly paper. He said that he began tithing at what seemed a most inopportune time. His family of five was living on the income he derived from a poorly-paying temporary job. They were deeply in debt. They couldn't afford a car.

Nevertheless, we made the break. We became a tithing family. God certainly proved to us that he meant it when he said that he would take care of our every need! However, the financial end of tithing is not the most important thing that God has done for me.

You see, I repented but I could not forgive myself for my sins, and so they dogged me. I could not pray. I could not trust in the Lord. I could not believe that I was a Christian. I was a failure financially and I could not understand the Bible. In church I could not sing the hymns of the church. I read the words but they did not apply to me. At communion I trembled and I felt awful. I went to the psychiatrists and they told me that I took religion too seriously.

By the grace of God I became a tither and the tide began to turn. I forgave myself for my past mistakes and the "dog pack" was called off.

I began to pray with inspiration and God began to answer my prayers. I began to trust Him. I came to believe that I was a Christian. My financial situation began to improve, for I went from a low-paying temporary job to a much higher-paying permanent job, and it continues to improve.

I began to understand the Bible. In church I now experience the presence of God, and it grows. I now sing the hymns of the church from the bottom of my heart, for the words are now significant to me; and at communion I experience something that I cannot explain.

In all my ways I try to acknowledge Him. I don't always do it, but I cannot separate tithing from that acknowledgement.[1]

Mr. Moore is just saying that Jesus told the truth when He 'taught, "Where your treasure is, there your heart will be also" (Matthew 6:21) and "Seek first his kingdom and his righteousness, and all these things will be given to you as well" (Matthew 6:33). It seems too good to be true, but it is a fact nevertheless. The practice of giving God the first ten percent of our earnings expresses, as nothing else in our money-dominated society does, that we really do believe in, trust in, and love God. In response, God keeps His promises. Tithing declares that the almighty God, and not the almighty dollar, holds first place in our hearts.

Like the Corinthian and Macedonian Christians, having given ourselves to the Lord *we will eagerly give ourselves to the work and the people of the Lord.* Even in their poverty the Macedonians gave generously to the Jewish Christians in Jerusalem whom they had never met. The more prosperous Corinthian Christians joined them in this charity. Christians everywhere are noted both for their regular tithing and their quick response to special appeals like this one. Whether the need is to relieve famine-stricken people in Africa or to resist leading someone astray in America, Christians join together to do what is best for others.

Baseball's Alvin Dark provides a good example. In 1949, shortly after he was traded by the Braves to the Giants, he was one of several team members approached by a cigarette company soliciting endorsements for their product. For the use of Dark's name in advertising the company offered five hundred dollars. He explained that as a Christian he believed smoking and drinking were very harmful to most people, and he didn't want to influence anybody to begin these habits, so he turned down their proposal. Some of his teammates were puzzled that he would turn his back on an easy five hundred like that. Players' salaries then were only a fraction of what they are now.

The next day Leo Durocher the Giant's manager in those days, called Dark into his office to tell him that he had been appointed team captain that year. With the appointment came a sum of money: exactly five hundred dollars.

I am not repeating this story to suggest that every time you take a stand for your Christian principles you can expect a payoff like this one. What is significant is Dark's explanation. He believes that because of the mighty promises of the Bible, "we Christians are freed from the tight-fisted, fearful miserliness of the world around us. We are sons of the One who owns the universe, and every source of earth and heaven can be released in our assistance if He chooses."[2] He explains that he was brought up as a tither. He sometimes found it hard to give five cents out of fifty when he had to get up before dawn to pedal around his paper route, but he did it. Now, he testifies, he has learned that you can never outgive God.

That has been my experience, too. By expressing my love for and faith in God through my tithes and additional offerings, I have participated in His work and had the joy of helping His people. That should be repayment enough. But in addition, God has materially blessed so that I find I cannot ever give faster than He does.

This has taught me something about the *grace of giving.* Not only have we been saved by God's grace, receiving favors from Him that we don't deserve, but He has enabled us to be generous in contributing to His work on earth—which has in turn given us a deeper experience of His grace. (One of the unexpected bonuses is freedom from the tyranny of the dollar!) God makes it possible for us to do what we would not do on our own. Christian stewardship seems unreasonable to someone who doesn't really know the Lord. "You mean you just throw away ten percent of your income?"

Even some Christians have difficulty bringing the whole tithe to the Lord (as did the Jews before them—see Malachi 3:6-11). Somebody wrote out "the devil's reasons for not tithing." Do his arguments sound persuasive? The devil says you can't tithe:

In January because of Christmas bills due.
In February because of fuel bills and car upkeep.
In March because of income taxes.
In April because of clothes for Easter.
In May because too much rain threatens the crops.
In June because too little rain threatens the crops.
In July because of vacation expenses coming up.
In August because of vacation expenses coming up.

In September because of the children's school needs.
In October because of winter clothes and doctor bills.
In November because of the Thanksgiving trip.
In December because of the Christmas shopping.

In the devil's list there is no room for the enabling grace of God and certainly no freedom from the tyranny of the almighty dollar. There is certainly, however, a clear indication of the devil's priorities. They are attractive ones. We have to choose whether they will be ours or not.

Management of our money is in fact the clearest statement we make of our true values. Godfrey Davis wrote a fine biography of the Duke of Wellington, who defeated Napoleon at the Battle of Waterloo. The author attributed his advantage over earlier biographers to the fact that he had found an old account ledger that showed how the duke spent his money. He said it was a far better clue to what Wellington thought was really important than Davis could find in reading his letters and speeches. (Remember Jesus? "Where your treasure is, there your heart will be also.")

Nothing gives us away as much as our check stubs. This is why the Bible stresses money management so strongly. If we really love the Lord and walk by faith in Him, our money will prove it. What we do with our money expresses what we really believe.

Paul doesn't command the Corinthian Christians to contribute to his special offering, but he wants "to test the sincerity of your love by comparing it with the earnestness of others" (2 Corinthians 8:8). Generosity is the proof of their love.

Jesus offered the same proof to us. "For you know the grace of our Lord Jesus Christ, that though he was rich, yet for your sakes he became poor so that you through his poverty might become rich" (2 Corinthians 8:9).

Paul has made three appeals here:

First, he appeals to the Macedonian example of joyful giving even in poverty.

Second, he appeals to the Corinthians' good beginning; they have started to collect an offering for Jerusalem and now should finish what they have started.

Third, he appeals to the example of Jesus himself. He gave all His riches for our sake. That's love.

Discussion Starters for Small Groups

How do you respond to this quotation from Marya Mannes: "The itch for things . . . is in effect a virus draining the soul of contentment"? Is this true for you?

How is our use of money indicative of our priorities in life?

Using this measure, what are your priorities?

What motivates you to give to God?

How do you describe how much to give?

Are you more likely to choose to alter your lifestyle so that you can purchase some item you want or to give more to the work of the church? Why?

What one thing do you think God would say to you about your use of financial resources?

CHAPTER EIGHT

Profiting Through God's Economics

2 Corinthians 9:6-15

The grace of giving is so vital to our growth—and so vigorously resisted by the vast majority of us—that we need to continue our thinking about the subject. In the Scripture before us, the apostle Paul concludes his appeal to the Christians at Corinth with a principle that, if applied, cannot fail to produce a happier more profitable life. It is so straightforward, so obvious, so logical a doctrine that we can only marvel at our stubborn rejection of it.

How to Produce a Good Profit
2 Corinthians 9:6

This is it: If you want to reap much, you sow much. If you want to earn a lot, you invest a lot. We translate this truism variously: "There ain't no free lunch." "No workee no monee." Paul takes his principle from agriculture: If you want a bountiful harvest, you bountifully sow the seed. "Whoever sows sparingly will also reap sparingly, and whoever sows generously will also reap generously."

He could have taken the same truth from the business world. A man who invests a hundred dollars in an account bearing ten percent interest can expect to earn ten dollars during the year he leaves it on deposit. The hundred thousand dollar investor will earn ten thousand. There is no inequity in the different totals. The generous investor has earned the more generous return.

The Bible frequently repeats this theme, applying it to the rewards of generosity. Here are some of my favorites:

One man gives freely, yet gains even more;
another withholds unduly, but comes to poverty.
A generous man will prosper;
he who refreshes others will himself be refreshed.
                                            —Proverbs 11:24, 25

He who is kind to the poor lends to the Lord
and he will reward him for what he has done.
                                            —Proverbs 19:17

Give, and it will be given to you. A good measure, pressed down, shaken together and running over will be poured into your lap. For with the measure you use, it will be measured to you.   —Luke 6:38

Do not be deceived: God cannot be mocked. A man reaps what he sows. The one who sows to please his sinful nature, from that nature will reap destruction; the one who sows to please the Spirit, from the Spirit will reap eternal life.   —Galatians 6:7, 8

Put all these Scriptures together and you come to the same conclusion: In your spiritual life, generous giving leads to generous growth.

Not long ago a woman vented her wrath against God on me. "I'm sorry, Mr. Minister" she exploded, "but I just don't understand why God likes some of us better than others." She left no doubt that she considered herself one of the "others." I know her life history pretty well. She has had some very difficult years. Yet as she took out her bitterness against God on me, I couldn't help thinking of many people I know who have survived worse afflictions than hers. They don't hate God. They praise Him.

What makes the difference?

"The one who sows to please his sinful nature, from that nature will reap destruction." "God loves a cheerful giver." I tried to recall any instances of this woman's giving. I knew that she had often been forced to serve the needs of her family, but I also knew how she resented having to do it. She was not a cheerful giver. She felt abused and unappreciated. Even at that moment she was angry because once again her freedom had been curtailed by an ailing parent. She was conscientiously doing her duty, but she was hating it. She believed that it was time for her to do what she wanted for herself. More than anything else, she wanted to please herself.

The consequences were inevitable: She was displeasing herself. She was reaping her own form of "destruction."

Yet I knew many, many others who in similar circumstances radiated a peace and joy that would baffle my friend. She would be certain that they could never have suffered as much as she. They were luckier, had better breaks, had more money, were born under different stars—or something!

The Scripture has a different explanation: "A man reaps what he sows"!

How, then, does a person produce a profitable life? By giving freely of oneself and one's resources, and then trusting God to bless. First give, then receive. First invest, then profit. But you must invest in what has true value.

George Buttrick has told somewhere of a congregation in Korea that lost its church bell when its village was captured during one of that country's many wars. The bell's metal was melted down for cannon. The villagers were very poor; they had no watches or clocks. Without their bell, there was nothing to call them to worship. The church elders prayed to God for a new church bell. Then one of the elders explained that he had been apprenticed to a bell-caster as a boy, but that he had forgotten the formula. The elders again prayed, asking God to remind their brother of the forgotten formula.

He then recalled enough of the formula so that he was able to cast a bell. When other villages heard of its excellent tone, they asked him to cast bells for them as well. Once more the elders met in prayer, this time asking God to guide their brother in the proper use of his unexpected income. After praying together they suggested that he use his money to send a missionary to Formosa, which he did.

Notice the order of events these wise elders presided over: First they went to the Lord with their need; then they accepted the generous gift of the bell-casters talent; then God blessed the man's generous giving with an opportunity to make money with his newly discovered talent; and finally the prayerful elders counseled him in the proper use of his profit. This enabled him to enlarge the impact of his generosity.

He sowed generously; he reaped generously; he sowed more generously, giving as the Lord prospered him (1 Corinthians 16:2).

How to Please God
2 Corinthians 9:7

We notice that Paul does not value the gift in itself; he specifically rejects anything given grudgingly. "God loves a cheerful giver" not one who reluctantly parts with his money or complains that he has been forced to give. Remember the proverb: "He who is kind to the poor lends to the Lord." God cares about the condition of our hearts. Kindness that results in giving, not the dollars in themselves, pleases God.

When Temple B'nai Emet hauled three of its contributors into court to collect their unpaid pledges, the court found in favor of the temple and against its delinquent members (who claimed they had left the temple, so shouldn't have to pay). It was the opinion of the court that the pledges were legally binding, so the defendants were ordered to pay.

That may be an effective way to collect money, but it definitely violates the spirit of Scriptural stewardship. The temple valued the dollars to be collected above the spirit in which the gifts were to be given.

Temples and churches sometimes lose their balance over finances. The costs of operating today's religious institutions have so skyrocketed that it is a rare institution that does not have to appeal to its members for more faithful giving. Unfortunately, many appeals are based on the institution's need to receive instead of the believer's need to give. We talk much about the advantages of giving and the blessings that come to a giver but how many of us really feel a deep need to give? Notice how frequently in Paul's appeal he speaks of the donor:

This act of grace on your part (8:6).
As you excel in everything see that you also excel in this grace of giving (8:7).
I want to test the sincerity of your love (8:8).
Finish the work (8:11).
If the willingness is there, the gift is acceptable according to what one has, not according to what he does not have (8:12).
The concern I have for you (8:16).
Show these men the proof of your love (8:24).
I know your eagerness to help (9:2).
That you may be ready (9:3).

More of Paul's comments about the donors will be noted as we study the rest of this chapter. What is impressive in his appeal is how little he has to say about the desperate need of the Jerusalem Christians to receive the offering, but how imperative it is that the Corinthian Christians give it. Theirs is the more critical need, since "it is more blessed to give than to receive." Paul obviously believes with Jesus that "where your treasure is, there your heart will be also." It is the heart God wants, not the gift. Do not expect to please God by any great display of almsgiving, any more than Jesus was impressed by the large amounts the rich threw into the temple treasury. It was the poor widow's all, you remember, that caught His attention (Mark 12:41-44).

It is the heart God wants—but the gift expresses the heart. Remembering this fact can steer us clear of two fatal mistakes well-meaning Christians sometimes make. The first is to believe that money itself is evil and thus to be avoided. Not money, but the love of money, is the evil.

> People who want to get rich fall into temptation and a trap and into many foolish and harmful desires that plunge men into ruin and destruction. For the love of money is a root of all kinds of evil. Some people, eager for money, have wandered from the faith and pierced themselves with many griefs.   —1 Timothy 6:9, 10

The second mistake is to believe that money is everything and therefore to be worshiped.

The Bible refutes both positions. Money is to be neither avoided nor worshiped. It is to be used. The cheerful giver finds joy in his generosity because in giving to the Lord's people and the Lord's causes he is worshiping the Lord with his money.

I read some time ago that for centuries Paris churches had a unique way of making their contributors (at least the male ones) cheerful in their giving. They selected the most beautiful and win-some woman in the city to hand around the collection purse for charities during the worship service. One woman was so beautiful it is reported, that people crowded the Church of St. Roche in order to be able to gaze at her as she pushed her way (assisted by two men rather burly, I suppose) through the crowd.

This is not exactly what Paul has in mind in mentioning God's love for cheerful givers. He merely calls our attention to the obvious fact that God—like us—loves to receive gifts given in cheerful love. Nobody takes pleasure in a begrudged gift.

How to Become Rich in Every Way
2 Corinthians 9:8-11

The promises Paul offers on behalf of God are extravagant:

"To make all grace abound to you"
"so that having all that you need"
"you will abound in every good work."
"[He] will also supply and increase your store of seed and will enlarge the harvest of your righteousness."
"You will be made rich in every way."

These extraordinary promises are not for everybody, but for the generous sower. Here Paul again sounds like his Lord:

Whoever can be trusted with very little can also be trusted with much, and whoever is dishonest with very little will also be dishonest with much. So if you have not been trustworthy in handling worldly wealth, who will trust you with true riches? And if you have not been trustworthy with someone else's property, who will give you property of your own? No servant can serve two masters. . . . You cannot serve both God and money.
—Luke 16:10-13

The road to true wealth is clearly marked. It begins with service to the God who owns everything, including money. The problem with choosing to serve money is that money doesn't own as much as God does, so cannot offer his servant what God promises His.

But God is a wise manager of His resources. He does not promote a submanager to a higher position until he has proved himself honest and trustworthy, nor will He raise an employee's pay until the worker has shown himself willing and loyal.

We must not misunderstand God here. It is quite possible to earn vast sums of money without serving God; worshipers of money know how to make money. But God promises that you will be rich in every way. Remember Jesus? "It is more blessed to give than to receive" (Acts 20:35). God has many riches in store for His generous people.

Bertrand Russell has exclaimed that it is "preoccupation with possession more than anything else that prevents men from living freely and nobly." There are so many examples of lives ruined by the pursuit of money that there is no need to amplify Russell's discovery. Let this one dismaying report be enough.

Carin Rubenstein writes in *Psychology Today* that this journal's survey shows that people's attitudes about their financial situation are more important than their actual net worth. Feelings of self-worth, job satisfaction, friendship, and personal growth matter more than having the highest income. "Simply stated," Rubenstein concludes, "the Money Contented rule their money rather than let it rule them."[1]

There were some discordant notes in the survey, however. Respondents were asked what they would be willing to do for a million dollars. Here are some results:

Have sexual relations once with a stranger:
76% of men, 58% of women would.
Marry someone I didn't love:
23% of men, 21% of women would.
Steal something:
21% of men, 10% of women would.

These are not exactly noble sentiments. These men and women could very well find themselves with one million dollars, but they would be far from "rich in every way."

Contrast their groveling with the nobility of two of my

friends on the mission field. When Doug and Marge Priest, Christian missionaries in Ethiopia, were driven out of that country by the communist revolution, they had just two hours to gather up their most precious possessions and leave. They selected three items: Doug's father's old Bible, their color slides, and Marge's mother's crocheted tablecloth. They walked away from all their other belongings, their vehicle, their house, everything. Was it hard? Of course. Was it a defeat? No, since their lives do not consist in the abundance of their possessions. (See Luke 12:13-21.) They had their freedom and their dignity. They also had their purpose in life: since they could not serve the Lord in Ethiopia, they would just transfer over to Kenya and keep on serving. They are rich in every way.

A skeptic could well raise an objection to the Bible's strong emphasis on giving, no matter how rich or poor you are. One wealthy Christian shared his story with a minister. He said he knew that many people explained away the large amounts of money he contributed to Christian causes by saying, "The reason he gives his money away is because he's got more than he can ever give away. He can talk stewardship because he has such a great fortune."

To the wealthy donor however his "explainers" had everything backward. He said that in the beginning he had nothing. He was just starting a law practice and had to support it (and his wife and child) by cleaning offices at night to pay bills. During this time he attended a missionary meeting. When an appeal was made to support the missionary's work, he put fifty dollars in the plate—the only money he had for the next two weeks. He had to go home and confess to his wife that they had no money for groceries or anything else for two weeks.

"What I'm trying to say to you," he told the minister "is that my fortune was amassed during the time I was giving my money away, not before. Before I die, I will have given away every cent of it."[2]

This man is rich in every way. He has learned that in

God's economics it is possible to give away and become richer.

But notice what Paul adds: "So that you can be generous on every occasion." God gives so that we can give. As we give more, God gives more, so that we can give more. Thus we are richer materially, and richer in joy and love and every other spiritual blessing.

How to Ensure a Bonus for Yourself
2 Corinthians 9:12-15

Paul can't stop. There is more yet. Note the bonuses he mentions:

Many expressions of thanks to God.
You have proved yourselves. (How important!)
Men will praise God for your obedience.
Men will praise God for your generosity. They will pray for you and learn to love you.

Here, then, is the road to the free and noble living that Bertrand Russell longs for. Your generosity proves your quality as nothing else can. You will enjoy, though you would never seek, true esteem in the eyes of your peers. More than esteem, you will experience their love and prayers.

My friend Bob Russell tells of one of his greatest memories of his days in his father's house. It was the occasion when his father, a factory worker went to the bank to borrow over two thousand dollars to give to his church to keep it from folding. Then he found a second job to pay back his loan. "Nothing my father ever said told me more about what was really important in his life." That was several years ago. The record of achievement amassed by Mr. Russell's several children is evidence enough to him that God's promise is true. His generosity on that and so many other occasions has brought the Russells every kind of riches, including that greatest treasure of all, the admiration of their own children.

Bob's story took me back to my childhood. In my home church in those days the offering tray was not passed. Instead we had boxes at the back of the meeting room. Members had to make a special effort to give something. It was really easy to sneak out without offering a penny to the Lord. I know. I mastered the technique.

But my father never did. One of my abiding—and repeated—memories is that of Dad stopping by the Lord's treasury box. It impressed me then; it impresses me now, because it was symbolic of his attitude toward God and life. He was a giver. God blessed his giving.

I preached in that church recently. Muriel Barlow wasn't there. Neither was Art. When I was still at home, the Barlows were there every Sunday, sitting in their same pew. I didn't know them well, but I knew they were there. They weren't obvious leaders, but they were faithful in their attendance. For several years Muriel was the church missions treasurer.

I knew about their attendance, but I didn't know about their giving. That was only made known later after they were gone. Art died first, and after his death Muriel kept up her attendance record, often walking the mile to the church come rain or shine—and in Tillamook, Oregon, it seemed in those days to be more rain than shine. When she died this quiet woman continued to give. Her will left all her estate to Christian endeavors: $54,211.08 to a Bible college and the same amount to her church.

Muriel Barlow is gone now, but her generosity lives after her. Because of her, young people are being educated for ministry and her church's outreach program has been extended further than before. When she was living, she had everything she needed and more. Through her giving, she has reaped a bonus of gratitude and praise to God.

Just one more word needs to be said, and Paul says it. "Thanks be to God for his indescribable gift!" He gave first; His gift was Jesus. All that we give pales by comparison. We won't try to compete with Him, then; we'll just thank Him—and with what He gives us, we'll imitate Him.

Discussion Starters for Small Groups

Were your parents generous? How has their attitude toward giving affected you?

Do you think Paul indicates in 2 Corinthians 9:6 that you will receive a dollar for every dollar you give? What is he saying?

How does your giving reflect righteousness?

How does God's gift affect your giving?

When is it difficult to give to others? When is it easy?

What is the best experience of giving that you remember?

Tell about a time when you received something that you needed from someone else. How did you feel? Was it easy to receive graciously? Why or why not?

What has God given you to share with others?

CHAPTER NINE

In the Beginning Is Thanks

Romans 1:16-25

Christian growth thrives on thanksgiving. A spirit of gratitude is not an option among Christians, to be exercised by a blessed elite upon whom life has smiled. Every Christian finds reason for thanksgiving, no matter what his lot. As the apostle Paul writes elsewhere "Be joyful always; pray continually; give thanks in all circumstances, for this is God's will for you in Christ Jesus" (1 Thessalonians 5:16-18). For Paul, giving thanks is as much a believer's obligation as faith in Christ is. "How do I do God's will?" asks the anxious Christian. For a starter, you can begin by giving thanks. In all circumstances. You won't find it an exercise in make-believe, either, because as a Christian you can know for certain that even in your present difficulty, "God works for the good of those who love him who have been called according to his purpose" (Romans 8:28). That's why Paul can write, "In all these things we are more than conquerors through him who loved us" (Romans 8:37).

The apostle returns to this theme again and again. In Colossians 3:15-17, for example, he writes this:

Let the peace of Christ rule in your hearts, since as members of one body you were called to peace. And be thankful. Let the word of Christ dwell in you richly as you teach and admonish one another with all wisdom, and as you sing psalms, hymns and spiritual songs with gratitude in your hearts to God. And whatever you do, whether in word or deed, do it all in the name of the Lord Jesus, giving thanks to God the Father through him.

"Be thankful." Sing "with gratitude in your hearts to God . . . giving thanks." Paul repeats himself so that we won't miss his message. Give thanks!

In the first chapter of Romans, a dark description of godless people, Paul dismisses any appeal that could be based on ignorance of God. The Lord has seen to it that we can know as much about Him as we need to know. His eternal power and His divine nature are evident; they always have been. But some people have haughtily turned their back on Him: "they neither glorified him as God nor gave thanks to him." The result has been disastrous for them: "Their thinking became futile and their foolish hearts were darkened."

It impresses me that the apostle couples thanklessness and futile thinking. Let's examine what this blighted union produces.

Ingratitude Darkens the Senses, Mind, and Worship
Romans 1:21-23

Before Samuel Liebowitz's career as a judge he was widely reputed for his skill as a criminal lawyer. He took on the tough cases, and usually won them. He is credited with rescuing seventy-eight men front the electric chair. Dale Carnegie used to impress his audiences with this fact from Liebowitz's life; then he would ask them how many of these men who owed their lives to their attorney ever stopped to thank him, or send a Christmas card? Carnegie would pause, then answer his own question: NONE. That's right, not one. Do you suppose there is any relationship between their thankless hearts and their troubles with the law?

Paul's writing suggests that there may be. Thanklessness, especially ingratitude toward God, clouds minds and darkens hearts. It certainly destroys relationships. Do you remember that well-worn yarn of the man who turned to his old friend to borrow some money? His friend turned him down flat. "But John," asked the surprised petitioner "how can you do this to me after all we have meant to each other? Have you forgotten that when we were in school I tutored you so that you would be able to pass your examinations? Or the time I saved you from drowning? Or when I gave you money to start your business, and when I talked your wife into marrying you?" "Yes," said John. "I remember all that. But what have you done for me lately?"

I'm afraid our prayers take on some of the same spirit, don't they? Instead of being flooded with praise to God for what He has already done, we can easily fall into a reproachful complaint, "But God what have you done for me lately?" Of such egoism is the kingdom of darkness.

We need to be reminded here that originally, *thanking* and *thinking* were the same word. *Thanking* evolved its separate existence quite naturally, since thanking is little more than right thinking. The right thinker gives thanks for what most people take for granted.

I recently had to chastise myself for thinking less gratefully than is good for me. I was participating in a national health survey. At the beginning of the hour-and-a-half interview, I was asked to rate my health on a scale from excellent to very poor. I checked *Fair*, since I am bothered by my share of aches and pains. Then we proceeded through the checklist of illnesses and physical complications: "Do you have diabetes, heart disease, any form of cancer, any of the several varieties of arthritis; sight or

hearing deficiencies, mental illness, respiratory difficulties," and so on through an incredible list of things like
hepatitis, malaria, yellow fever, and others. After a while,
when I consistently answered *No,* I was forced to tell my
interviewer, "You'd better change that *fair* to *good."* And I
gave thanks. I have too long concentrated on what's
wrong with my health; I have boorishly taken for granted
what is good about it.

My ingratitude hasn't stopped there. My blessings in-
clude plenty of good food and drink, more clothes than I
need, a well-equipped modern house, more modern con-
veniences than my grandparents could have dreamed of.
Add to these the variety and richness of our life's experiences, the loved ones we have and cherish, the miles we
have traveled and the sights we have seen. We must not
forget, either, the people who haven't cheated us, and the
friends who haven't deserted us even when we have given
them just cause.

Obviously my family and I need to say thanks to someone. The Someone is the Source of all these blessings, our
life's Partner. If we don't give thanks, if instead we take all
these blessings for granted, Paul is right—our minds will
become darkened, our thinking futile. In the end, we'll
prove ourselves mere fools.

When our friends Dave and Wanda McCord came home
at 8:30 one Saturday morning they were greeted by open
doors, open drawers, and scattered possessions everywhere. They had been out with their church kids and
couldn't get home until the teenagers they were supervis-
ing were ready to call it a night. The thieves had been
thorough. They had stolen the McCord's stereo, a movie
camera, a watch, some cash, and their locked box contain-
ing valuable documents and some bonds. At first Dave
and Wanda searched to discover what was missing; only
gradually did it dawn on them how much had not been
taken, how much they had to be thankful for in spite of
their loss.

Telling about this incident later, Dave quoted the famous

Bible scholar Matthew Henry, who was once robbed of his wallet. In that circumstance Henry, like the McCords, found reason to rejoice: "Let me be thankful first because I was never robbed before; second, because, although they took my purse, they did not take my life; third, because, although they took my all, it was not much; and fourth, because it was I who was robbed and not I who robbed."

Henry's comments are worth reading again, especially his third and fourth observations. I keep hoping I could demonstrate the same attitude.

I could, I think, if I would only remember what great wealth I have always enjoyed in life. Even now, as I am writing these words, I glance out the window from time to time, seldom thinking to give thanks for the beauty that looks back at me. My senses have eaten too well; they grow dull from their overindulgence.

I need the reminder of a passenger on a jetliner who was so enthralled by what he was seeing from his window seat that he kept exclaiming, "Wonderful, wonderful, wonderful." Finally his seat-mate couldn't keep quiet any longer. "How come you seem to be having the time of your life while the rest of us seem bored stiff with this flight?"

"Until a few weeks ago," the happy man answered, "I was almost completely blind. I could just barely tell day from night. But a very special operation gave me my sight, and now I'm seeing things that I've never seen before. What may seem so ordinary to you and the others is just out of this world for me."

That doesn't mean, either, that he had no cause to give thanks when he was blind. Joe Sizemore has taught me that. Blinded when he was a teenager, Joe says that he has been more blessed than cursed in his sightlessness. To name just one blessing, he has developed his other senses to a height that sighted people never achieve. He enjoys rich sensory experiences we will never know. So he gives thanks.

It's altogether too easy for us to miss so much of the wealth God has given us because, surrounded by it, we ignore it, dreaming of fortune elsewhere. We're like the fishes in the sea:

"Oh, where is the sea," the fishes cried,
As they swam the Atlantic waters through;
"We've heard of the sea and the ocean tide
And we long to gaze on its waters blue."

Evidence of God's providence lies all around us, too, as the waters of the ocean surround the curious fish. Yet we choose to focus on what's missing or unpleasant. So we grumble and gripe and deny, neither acknowledging God nor thanking Him. Turning away from Him, we puff ourselves up with our worldly wisdom, dub ourselves Wise Ones, worship our man-made gods fashioned after "mortal man and birds and animals and reptiles." In the end, we replace God's ways with our ways, with disastrous results:

Since they did not think it worthwhile to retain the knowledge of God, he gave them over to a depraved mind, to do what ought not to be done. They have become filled with every kind of wickedness, evil, greed and depravity. They are full of envy, murder, strife, deceit and malice. They are gossips, slanderers, God-haters, insolent, arrogant and boastful; they invent ways of doing evil; they disobey their parents; they are sense less, faithless, heartless, ruthless.

—Romans 1:28-31

The quickness with which ingratitude slips into gross immorality raises a question: Is it possible that we resist giving thanks to God because a thankful heart is an obligated heart? Whenever someone does something good to you, for which you are really grateful, what is your first impulse? "What can I do in return? How can I express my gratitude?" It's an automatic response, isn't it? Then what if that someone is God? What do you do then?

Walter Percy's thoroughly unadmirable hero in *Love in the Ruins* muses on just this moral dilemma. Divorced from his family, the dedicatedly selfish man is reflecting on the death of his daughter. There had been a chance to save her he believed, if he had taken her to Lourdes in time. But he hadn't. He didn't want to. He didn't he now admits to himself, because he was afraid she might be cured. "What then? Suppose you ask God for a miracle and God says yes, very well. How do you live the rest of your life?"[1]

How indeed?

Percy asks the right question. If you have cause to be grateful, and you are grateful, you will change. That's why thanksgiving is so important to one's spiritual growth and development.

Gratitude Brightens the Senses, Mind, and Worship
Romans 1:16, 17

A couple of years ago Jennifer Oakland was in the hospital. She was in the third grade, I think; anyway, she seemed pretty tiny in that big hospital bed. As soon as she returned home she sent me a thank-you card, which I still treasure. Inside she printed this:

Dear Lawsons, Thank you for coming to see me, Dr. Lawson. I liked the prayer you said. When I got out of the hospital I was very glad. The only part I didn't like was the IV taken out. Thank you for coming to see me. Love, Jennifer.

I want to be around Jennifer when she's an adult. If she has the appreciative spirit then that her parents are inspiring in her now, she'll be a wise and winsome woman. She is being taught to be grateful, even for small favors. Her attitude will brighten her life.

To understand the theology of the great apostle Paul, you need to begin with his attitude. Like Jennifer's, it is one that sparkles with gratefulness. That's why he is "not

ashamed of the gospel" and calls it "the power of God for
the salvation of everyone who believes." How could he be
ashamed of the power that turned his life around? (See
Acts 9.) So great was the transformation that Paul would
forever speak of the grace God lavished on him. He
couldn't get over God's kindness. God revealed himself to
Paul; what is left but for Paul, in word and deed, to give
thanks?

A very wise man once pointed out that all of the apostle
Paul's dogmas were doxologies before they became dogmas. A doxology is a song of praise and thanksgiving, and
a dogma is a teaching. To understand Paul, then, you
must trace his famous instructions to their source, gratitude to God. Even his ethical teachings devolve naturally
from Paul's belief that an upright life is the fitting expres-
sion of thanks to God. It is obvious that Paul's thankful
heart has brightened his mind. He urges the same on us;
it's essential for spiritual growth.

When Isaac Bashevis Singer was awarded the Nobel
Prize for fiction in 1978, the self-effacing writer was sev-
enty-four. His humility was shown in the way he received
the news of his award: "Are you sure?" he asked. Then
when a reporter asked what he would do with his prize
money and whether it would change his life-style, he
replied, "Everything will remain the same—same type-
writer, same wife, same apartment, same telephone number, same language. I am thankful, of course, for the
prize and thankful to God for each story, each idea, each
word, each day."[2]

In his gratitude, his mind has been lightened, and in his
eighth decade he can still receive fresh insights for writing. He is the embodiment of the spirit captured by an
older woman in "A Christmas Memory." The author recalls
a special holiday season from his childhood, made memo-
rable by the woman he calls simply "my friend." She bakes
for him, goes kite-flying with him, loves him as only a
grandmotherly woman can love a little boy.

There is an unforgettable moment when, as they play

their kites against the winter winds, she shares a glimpse she had just caught of eternal truth. She tells the boy that she has always thought you couldn't see the Lord until you were sick and dying. Then He would come in a dazzle, like the sun's rays piercing the colored glass in the Baptist church window. Now, suddenly, she realizes that that's not it at all. She's ready to bet that "the Lord has already shown himself" in things as they are around her. Seeing them is like seeing Him. "As for me, I could leave the world with today in my eyes."[3]

Her words might not have stopped me if Frona Ruetten hadn't come into my life, but thanks to her, I have known someone who left the world with today in her eyes. I still have a copy of the last letter she wrote her friends. It's dated January, 1980, and postmarked Ely, Nevada. She had gone there to be closer to her children.

Frona was a member of our congregation. When her husband died, although she was already in her sixties, she felt free to become what she had always wanted to be: a missionary. She volunteered to TCM, a Vienna-based mission agency serving Iron Curtain countries. They accepted her, undoubtedly because she offered to do the most menial tasks for them. She became the mission's laundress. Every summer for five years she traveled to Austria to take up her duties. The impact of this humble servant on the young people she served is incalculable.

She quit her work only when her body refused to go any longer. She returned to us in the fall of 1979 with a brain tumor. Surgery could not remove all of it. Frona realistically assessed her situation and chose to move to Ely, so she would be less a burden on her family.

When I print here some of this final letter, you will know why Frona seemed to so many of us to be an extraordinary woman. With little income, with what she considered few natural talents, yet with an eager and thankful spirit, she kept on growing until the day she died. I have walked through their final days with many people; I have tried to comfort some as they have railed against God, questioned their fate, given themselves up to bitterness, or resigned themselves to the inevitable. I have rejoiced with many Christians who were glad to be going to God. I have observed the difference Christ makes in dying as well as living. With Frona, the role of a grateful heart—grateful to God and others—shines through:

> I am truly grateful for your concern and love.
> It was a twelve and a half hour trip [from Mesa to Ely] but I was very comfortable on a foam rubber bed in the back of the wagon. To top it off we had a beautiful day.
> At this point I want to give thanks to my Heavenly Father for this precious privilege He has allowed me, for if this had not happened, I fear that I would not have been able to give myself entirely into His care. I want to thank Him for what He has done for me.

Then Frona expresses thanks for the doctors and nurses at the hospital, for opportunities to witness to God's love, for members of her church, for "flowers, fruit, letters, greetings of all sorts, visitations, and prayers." Then on to her friends from the X-B Trailer Ranch for all they did for her. She can't stop—she mentions the excellent care she is receiving in her Ely nursing home, then to all of her friends everywhere she says this:

> I wish I could respond personally for your kindness, but I cannot. I do well to feed myself with my left hand, but I am learning. Perhaps before too long, I will develop some dexterity in my left hand, as well as continue to regain some use of my right hand. My strength is increasing and I am able to help the nurses when they care for me.

Her litany continues with thanks to the mission agency, TCM, and to Gene Dulin, its director. Finally, she says:

I could not close this letter to each of you without telling you how grateful I am to my family. . . . My family has stood by me in this crisis either by telephone or being with me, and I am so grateful to my Heavenly Father for their devoted love during this time.

If Frona lived her long life as she died—and her friends tell me she did—then it is easy to account for her amazing power. She was a thankful person. Her gratitude opened her mind and heart, energized her service, and magnified her influence. It will do as much for us if we learn to take our troubles for granted and focus our attention on the good things we have.

Do not minimize this virtue. Psalm 95:2 exhorts us to come before the Lord with thanksgiving. There's no other way. Knowing God is not enough (Romans 1:21) if you don't give thanks to Him. Sometimes, in fact, only thanksgiving will hold you to God.

When a youthful G. K. Chesterton was struggling through higher education and finding his faith attacked on every side, he said later, he "hung on to religion by one thin thread of thanks."[4] It was enough.

Charles Colson recalls a moment from his preconversion days that helped pave the way, although Colson was not conscious of it, for his later turn toward the Lord. He and his ten-year-old son were boating. As the father sat in the boat watching "the joy of discovery in his eyes, the thrill of feeling the wind's power in his hands," Colson found himself talking to God. He can still recall the exact words. "Thank You, God, for giving me this son, for giving us this one wonderful moment. Just looking now into this boy's eyes fulfills my life. Whatever happens in the future, even if I die tomorrow, my life is complete and full. Thank You."

It shook him up a little afterwards when he realized that he had been talking to God, since he was not a believer! He had not even admitted the existence of God. In that moment, however, his gratitude overflowed. It had to be expressed. To Someone. He was inching toward God. His conversation assumed that "personal communication with this unproved God was possible. Why else would I have spoken, unless deep down I felt Someone, somewhere, was listening?"[5]

When Colson later gave himself to Christ, he did so as the logical conclusion of his feelings of gratitude. With him, as with Paul, doxology (thanksgiving) led to dogma (teaching based on belief).

Do you want to grow in Christ? May I suggest that the best place to begin is not with a study of some theological tome. Start rather with you. With your attitude. Do you have a grateful heart? Do you give thanks often? Regularly? In all circumstances?

Start right now. Let your gratitude to God enlighten your heart and mind and worship.

Discussion Starters for Small Groups

What are some of the consequences of an unthankful spirit?

Paul encouraged the Thessalonians to "give thanks in all circumstances." Do you find this advice easy to follow?

How are thanksgiving and contentment related?

When do you have the most difficulty following Paul's advice on giving thanks?

What could you do that would help you give thanks even in these difficult circumstances?

CHAPTER TEN

The Best Knife
for This Operation

2 Timothy 3:10-17

You have probably wondered why, in a book on the subject of Christian growth and development, I didn't start with the obvious. Everybody knows that if you are going to grow spiritually, you have to spend time in God's Word. Why didn't I start there?

I chose to wait until this chapter because it isn't good enough just to open the Bible and expect it somehow to grow the reader up. We have to approach God's Word with an open mind and heart. Our thinking (a close kin of thanking, remember) must be right.

I think we're ready now. We've swept aside the proud, unforgiving, selfish, and irresponsible spirit that often blocks a Christian's progress, and we've learned to center our lives on Christ in a trusting, relaxed, generous, and grateful attitude. With this kind of preparation on our part, God's Word can do its part.

To guide our meditation on the value of Bible study, we'll use the New Testament's most famous statement about Scripture, 2 Timothy 3:10-17. The apostle Paul's instruction to his younger colleague Timothy is as relevant to us as it was to him. Paul tells him to imitate good models, to study the Scriptures, and to equip himself for every good work. To us he would say, "Go thou and do likewise." So let's take time for a little study of those three things Paul told Timothy (and tells us) to do—and then let's go and do them with enthusiasm. We may be surprised by the joy we find.

Imitate Good Models
2 Timothy 3:10-14
Paul doesn't hesitate to offer himself as an example worthy of imitation. With a confidence few of us could muster he calls Timothy's attention to

"my teaching"
"my way of life"
"my purpose"
"[my] faith, patience, love, endurance"
"the persecutions I endured."

At Antioch of Pisidia, a town in southern Asia Minor, Paul and Barnabas preached in the synagogue on their first missionary journey, but their messages so offended the local Jews that they drove the missionaries from the city to Iconium, then drove them out of that town. At Lystra they stirred up a mob that stoned Paul and dragged him outside the city, leaving him for dead. Preaching the gospel was no piece of cake in those days! "Yet," Paul hastens to add, "the Lord rescued me from all of them (verse 11)."

Nor would the veteran preacher have Timothy think that his is a unique experience. "In fact, everyone who wants to live a godly life in Christ Jesus will be persecuted, while evil men and imposters will go from bad to worse, deceiving and being deceived." Shall we be frightened, or challenged?

If it is the fate of Christians to be persecuted, and it is, then it is imperative that younger believers in Christ observe and imitate older models. Paul does not call attention to himself in order to boast of his steadfastness, but to prove that loyalty to the Lord is possible even under the most adverse condition—and that the Lord can be counted on to take care of His own.

Of course Paul is not the only role model that Timothy has. Earlier in this letter the apostle writes, "I have been reminded of your sincere faith, which first lived in your grandmother Lois and in your mother Eunice and, I am persuaded, now lives in you also." Blessed is the man who has godly parents and grandparents. Belief in Christ came quickly to Timothy because of them. No righteous son of righteous parents can fail to benefit from their example.

On the solid foundation of his mother's and grandmother's piety and his own demonstration of faithfulness, Paul then urges Timothy to "continue in what you have learned and have become convinced of, because you know those from whom you learned it, and how from infancy you have known the holy Scriptures."

My daughter is now studying at our state university. It's not high school, she has discovered to her dismay. It's not church, either! Almost daily her belief in God is being knocked about by brilliant enemies of the faith. Growing up in a Christian home, she has not had to marshall facts and arguments to defend positions that are taken for granted by our family. How can I help her? Will she survive as a believer?

In our frequent talks, more than once I have used Paul's quiet suggestion here. You know the people from whom you learned the Scriptures. They are trustworthy. Now your beliefs are being bombarded by learned strangers. What do you know about them? What is the effect of their anti-God position on their ethics, on their world view, on their behavior in general? Are they trustworthy people? Test their teachings in the laboratory of life. Be sure you know where they are going before you follow them.

A healthy skepticism is a valuable tool for a university student. "By their fruits you shall know them" can be spoken of more than the Pharisees. By their fruits Timothy had learned to trust his mother and grandmother. When they taught the Scriptures to him he was prepared to listen, because they had never led him astray before. Nor had Paul.

When I was chairman of English at Milligan College I was responsible for recommending new professors for the department. What a revealing exercise that was! I'll never forget one young man whose interview did not go very well. I was somewhat surprised when he chastised me for what he called my "missionary" attitude to my students. I guess he found me to be a bit "preachy." He probably did not regret that we refused to hire him, however, because he told me in our conversation that he really preferred teaching in a large university to doing so in a small college. He didn't want to get close to his students. He wanted to be able to lecture to one or two hundred students and walk out of their lives. He wanted no involvement. He had already learned how difficult it is to teach in an environment when your teaching is tested by the quality of your life. He just wanted to live and let live, to teach in academic isolation.

Such isolation was not possible for Paul. He was teaching the stuff of life. If it was truth, it could be lived. If it was lived, Timothy could imitate the one who lived it.

Paul's advice is still good.

Study the Scriptures
2 Timothy 3:14-16

More than imitation is needed, however. If right thinking is our concern, then we have to feed that thinking with nourishment from above. Jesus fended off the devil's clever lure ("If you are the Son of God, tell these stones to become bread") and emerged from His struggle victorious because He had filled himself with Scripture: "Man does not live on bread alone, but on every word that comes from the mouth of God" (Matthew 4:3, 4). There is no substitute for Bible study.

Your word is a lamp to my feet
and a light for my path.
* * * * * * * * * * * * * * * * * * * *
I have hidden your word in my heart
that I might not sin against you.

−Psalm 119:105, 11

Ask almost any Christian and he'll tell you how valuable Bible study is. Ask him how much time he spends in the Word of God and he'll turn strangely silent. The truth is, the Bible is much more admired than read−to the shame of the church. How can we excuse ourselves for ignoring words that are "able to make you wise for salvation through faith in Christ Jesus"? Not too long ago TV preacher Bob Schuller (of the famous Crystal Cathedral in California) sponsored a Gallup poll on Bible knowledge. Only forty-six percent of all the respondents could name the first four books of the New Testament. Even worse, some answered that religion was very important to them, but even among them only fifty-six percent could correctly name Matthew, Mark, Luke, and John. Can everyone in our church name them?

Other questions were also revealing. Seventy percent knew where Jesus was born (thanks to the popularity of Christmas), but only forty-two percent could name the preacher of the Sermon on the Mount. Perhaps we can take some comfort in the fact that in 1954 the scores on a similar survey were six to nine points lower on each question. But how do we reconcile these low scores with the claim of eighty-one percent of these respondents that they are Christians, and the fact that sixty percent of those surveyed believed that belief in Jesus as Savior is absolutely necessary for someone to truly know God?

How important is an understanding of the Bible? What other source of information about Jesus do we have? What other compendium of God's words do we have? Where else can we learn what God is like or what He wants? Is there any excuse for Biblical ignorance? Is there any substitute for Bible knowledge?

The Scriptures are "able to make you wise," as Paul writes to Timothy. I like what Malcolm Muggeridge has written in *Jesus Rediscovered*. When asked whether he is a Christian, Muggeridge sometimes wants to disclaim any association with church, especially when he listens to the Archbishop of Canterbury addressing the House of Lords on some moral question, or when he tunes in to some radio or television evangelist. He would rather not be associated with the likes of such. But when he reads books like Tolstoy's *Resurrection* or Dostoyevsky's *Brothers Karamazov* or becomes absorbed in the music of Bach, or when he reads Pascal or admires Chartres Cathedral, he is drawn to the Christian way of looking at life. Then when he turns to the Gospels and Epistles, he finds them "irresistibly wonderful." "Is it not extraordinary to the point of being a miracle," he asks, that this loosely constructed narrative even in an antique translation, should after so many centuries "still have power to quell and dominate a restless, opinionated, over-exercised and under-nourished twentieth-century mind?"[1] It wouldn't be surprising to Paul. In the first century he had already discovered the Scriptures to be "able to make you wise."

I quote Muggeridge because for many years this highly intelligent, well-educated writer fought against the Bible's claim on his life. He didn't want to be a Christian or to be associated with Christians. He preferred his curled-lip cynicism, his clever arrogance, his sophisticated sparring with a jaded society. But he couldn't stay away from God's Word. It was, as he said, "irresistibly wonderful." It changed him. This member of the intelligentsia learned that he who had boasted of his vast learning could not claim to be educated if he did not know the Bible—and knowing the Bible diminished the importance of all other learning. "Every word that comes from the mouth of God" devalues all words spoken against it.

The Scriptures will change anyone who gives them a chance. They are "God-breathed," inspired. As God breathed into man the breath of life (Genesis 2:7), so He breathed life into the words of His Word.

What are Scriptures good for? Beware lest you be fooled. They are not mere pretty platitudes to brighten a cloudy day. Nor are they magical. You don't close your eyes and open to any page and expect to put your finger on a verse to rule you for the day. There's danger in such childish use of this mature volume. Don't let any enthusiastic media preacher convince you that if you just memorize this or that Scripture all your troubles will be over. Paul becomes very specific: God designed the Scriptures for "teaching, rebuking, correcting, and training in righteousness." We return to our theme: God is doing everything He can to help His people grow up. Like the loving Father He is, He gives instructions to help us mature.

"Teaching" we accept, but "rebuking" is a sterner word. It suggests that when we get out of line the Scriptures can call us back to order. When you seriously study the Bible, you are less likely to get sentimental about it. Sometimes it stings. Amy Carmichael, the great missionary to India's women and children, has written, "If you have never been hurt by a word from God, it is probably that you have never heard God speak." She's right. "Those whom I love I rebuke and discipline" the Lord tells the church in Laodicea (Revelation 3:19) as He urges them to "be earnest, and repent." Of course He does. No truly loving parent heaps unmixed praise on a child. Rebuking and discipline are as much a part of the teaching process as praise and encouragement. Then, when the child is older, the words of his youth continue to guide.

Children nurtured on God's Word will likewise be guided by its teaching all the days of their lives. There was a young man of Lancaster, Pennsylvania, who thought he would be the exception. When he volunteered for service in the Green Berets, he was turned down. The officers discovered that he had been raised in the Church of the Brethren, a historic peace church.

"But," he protested, "I am not a pacifist. I reject that part of my religious background."

They didn't believe him, and they wouldn't accept him. They had learned from past experience, they explained, that his religious background would have a lasting influence on him. There would be a time when, as a matter of conscience, he would refuse to obey an order. "We cannot afford for that to happen," they told him.

He protested, but they didn't budge. So he went into the regular army.

By the way, when he was stationed in Germany, he was given an order that he and several friends refused to obey. It went against his conscience. He had not rejected that part of his Church of the Brethren heritage after all.

You cannot escape. When I was teaching in college, my wife teased me. For six years I had ministered to a church before accepting an assignment as a college professor of English. I regularly taught at least one of my classes in our house, where Joy could sit in with us from time to time. She wrote to friends in our former church. "Roy is still preaching; he has just changed the text."

She was right. I found that when I was teaching literature, I was still thinking Bible. My thought patterns, my point of view, my illustrations, and my source of inspiration were Biblical. Try as I might, I could not leave my religious background behind.

I know of no more powerful book. I'm not alone in this belief, by the way. In 1979 a Soviet-Finnish customs agreement went into effect, listing dangerous items that could no longer be imported. The prohibited items: whiskey, weapons, drugs, and the Bible. What explosive company the Scriptures sometimes keep!

C. H. Spurgeon, the powerful preacher of nineteenth-century London, tells of a seedy character who went to hear the evangelist George Whitefield. He didn't go to learn but to mock. He memorized Whitefield's sermon and mastered his imitation of the preacher's style. Then he delivered it to his militantly non-Christian buddies. In the middle of his mockery, however, he suddenly stopped. He couldn't go on. His heart was broken. He found that, in spite of himself, his preaching of Whitefield's sermon converted him. Later this scoundrel became far better known as Mr. Thorpe of Bristol, who led many people to Christ. The message of the gospel corrected him! Like a surgeon with a skilled knife, Mr. Whitefield had wielded the Word of God to cut away his critic's ridicule and hypocrisy. Then the Spirit could convict him of the truth.

Dr. L. Nelson Bell's well-known parable of two surgeons comes to mind here.[2] Surrounded by the hospital residents, these two highly-skilled, eminently honored surgeons, one of them the hospital's chief of staff, stood motionless in their sterilized gowns and caps as the anesthetic began taking effect on the patient stretched out before them.

Beside the table were the instrument stands holding clamps, clips, retractors, spreaders, scissors, and sutures of various kinds. The surgeons examined the instruments, taking them up one by one. They hovered over the patient; they marked the place where the incision would ordinarily be made. But they did not cut. They used no knife.

After about an hour, the patient was rolled into the recovery room, then later on into his room. Friends sent flowers and messages. The doctors checked in on him from day to day. But he didn't improve. He complained of the same old pain. His condition deteriorated. Finally the hospital conducted an investigation.

At the staff meeting, a resident timidly questioned the Chief of Staff. He had scrubbed in on several of these unsuccessful surgeries, he said, and he noticed the same thing in each one of them. The surgeon did not use the knife. There was no incision, no bleeding, nothing removed. The patient went out of the operating room the same as he came in.

The chief surgeon quickly defended their procedures. Their knife was old, full of imperfections, not to be trusted. It was better used as an ornament, something suitable to keep on the table, perhaps, but not effective in today's complicated surgical conditions.

His explanation sounded plausible. But patients did not get better. They needed the knife. "The word of God is living and active," the Bible says. It is "sharper than any double-edged sword; it penetrates even to dividing soul and spirit, joints and marrow; it judges the thoughts and attitudes of the heart" (Hebrews 4:12). We need the knife.

Of course to need it is not to want it. Most of us would quickly agree with one honest Christian who admitted that many believers don't really want to know what the Bible actually says, because the minute we know it we become responsible for doing it. We far prefer hearing holy sounds to having to respond to the Bible's demanding ideas.

Study to Equip Yourself for Every Good Work
2 Timothy 3:17

But if we don't know the Bible what use are we in God's kingdom? Paul reminds Timothy (and us) that the "man of God" is to be "thoroughly equipped for every good work" (verse 17). Bible study is not an end in itself; we are not called to be students but to be workers. Studying is preparation for labor.

Every university has its legion of perpetual students. Year after year these poor lost souls enroll in classes (or just hang around the real students), reading, absorbing, debating, and sponging. They don't intend to go to work; they are students only.

Unfortunately, more churches than we like to admit carry far too many perpetual students on their rolls. Faithful in worship attendance, even in Sunday school, they are great hearers of the word but doers never. When Dawson Trotman, who founded The Navigators organization, was trying to recruit counselors for a Billy Graham

Crusade in a large city, he called many of the supporting churches in search of workers. "Could we have the names of the men and women in your congregation who know their Bibles well enough to lead someone to Christ?" he asked them.

The church secretary of one of the larger congregations asked him to repeat the qualification again.

He did. Then, after a long pause, she answered, "You know, we did have a man like that in church once, but he moved away."[3]

What will the Lord make of a group of Christians who have met for years and years, yet who cannot raise up a host of people able and ready to share the best news in the world with others who haven't heard it yet?

The minister of one such congregation finally gave vent to his exasperation with his people's vast ignorance of the Bible. He announced that one Sunday evening the congregation would vote on what portions of the Bible should be left in and what portions should be taken out on the basis of what they had read. The portions the majority of the members had read during the past year would be left in; what the majority had not read would be removed. It was a traumatic evening for the congregation; their reconstructed Bible contained Genesis 1, the Ten Commandments from Exodus, one or two favorite passages from Isaiah, the twenty-third Psalm, excerpts from the Sermon on the Mount the third and fourteenth chapters of John, and 1 Corinthians 13. That's all.

The congregation got the preacher's point. "It is not the Bible believed but the Bible believed and read which has the potential for changing lives."[4] One woman, by the way, was irate. She scolded her preacher for tearing up God's Holy Word in front of the church. She did not seem to be upset that so little of the Word was holy to her brethren.

God intends the Bible to equip people for good work.

In our church we are doing everything we can to help our members know and apply God's Word. Of course we provide Sunday school for every age group. The sermons are careful studies of portions of Scripture. We make aids available for personal and family devotions. In addition to the regular Sunday-school classes we also offer a wide variety of elective classes for adults. Each week dozens of Bible studies meet in the homes of our members. We encourage our people to study as if their life depends on it— as it does.

Our goal is not Bible study, but the developing of a host of Christians fully equipped to be able to do every good work God wants of us. The Lord wants skilled surgeons operating on His behalf. The Bible is the best knife God has given us for this kind of operation.

Discussion Starters for Small Groups

How frequently do you study the Bible?

How does your rate of spiritual growth compare with the frequency of your Bible Study?

How do you respond to Amy Carmichael's comment that "if you have never been hurt by a word from God, it is probably that you have never heard God speak"?

In what ways has Scripture taught you?
                              rebuked you?
                              corrected you?
                              trained you?

What one thing can you do that would most improve your study of God's Word?

CHAPTER ELEVEN

Powerful and Effective Prayer

James 5:13-16

Nothing is more threatening for many new Christians than the subject of prayer. They know they are supposed to pray regularly, but they don't know how. They hear testimonies from seasoned prayer warriors who speak of their joy and power in prayer, but these young believers don't experience either when they pray. They have been told they can't grow spiritually without a strong prayer life, but they don't know how to begin.

If this is your feeling, then why don't we begin with the best example of a prayer life we can find: with the ministry of Jesus. Pressed by responsibilities on every hand, Jesus periodically excuses himself from the pushing crowds and leaves for a retreat into solitude and prayer.

We already imitate Him in one regard: We too are pressed by our responsibilities. How can we meet all the daily demands on us and grow spiritually at the same time?

Why not imitate Jesus? He was under severe stress, yet

He handled His pressures by taking periodic retreats for solitude and prayer.

Solitude

I make this suggestion cautiously, because I may be misunderstood. Too much withdrawal from society is a dangerous thing. Some eyes reading this page have already grown dim from too quiet a life. You've been retreating from people for too long. You've been hurt and you are licking your wounds; you've worked hard and are worn out and you have vowed never to let people take advantage of you like that again; you've sacrificed all you're going to sacrifice for the sake of other people.

If you've been thinking these thoughts lately, my emphasis on solitude is poison for you. You don't need to hide anymore and you certainly don't need any more justification for hiding. You will wither and die if you don't get back into action as a helpful member of your church. Jesus made occasional retreats—but only to regain strength to fulfill His obligations. He did not hold himself aloof from those who needed Him.

This chapter is intended for the overworked, underrested, super-charged individual who, like Jesus, is concerned about the needs of others and constantly giving to meet those needs.

Reading through the Gospel of Mark, I paused at 6:45, 46. "Immediately Jesus made his disciples get into the boat and go on ahead of him to Bethsaida, while he dismissed the crowd. After leaving them, he went into the hills to pray." This isn't the first time Mark mentions the Lord's temporary escape from the multitudes. See 1:35; 4:35; 6:30, 31. I noted this one especially, however because of the miraculous events that surround it.

On the one side is Jesus' feeding of the five thousand. What an expenditure of energy that must have been! Hours of teaching huge crowds of people, then the miracle. Mark says it was "immediately" after this that Jesus took His retreat.

But the retreat was followed quickly by His rescue of the disciples straining against the storm on the Sea of Galilee (Mark 6:47-51). This in turn was followed by the strenuous healing of countless numbers of people on the western coast of the lake (Mark 6:53-56). Is it any wonder that Jesus sometimes had to get off by himself to be re-charged?

When you find yourself harassed and worn out, do you imitate the Master? Can you get away, by yourself, to get in touch with God? Nothing has helped me more than what I call my "minute vacations." When I can't remove myself from the scene physically, I can at least stop to enjoy the scene: a pause to appreciate a brilliant sunset, or to smell a tiny flower, or to whisper a word of thanks to God. Just a moment.

I was amused a few years ago when trend setters were all agog over their newly practiced periods of meditation. They thought they had discovered something new. Fascinated by gurus imported from the Hindu East, they were devoting their fifteen minutes every morning and afternoon to disciplined solitude. They emptied their minds, they concentrated on their secret mystical syllable, and they boasted to the world that they were changed people.

Christians have enjoyed solitary meditation for centuries. Jesus practiced it. So have His disciples.

The art has been dangerously threatened in recent years, perhaps, as our complicated modern life-style has shoved it aside. We seem almost to fear quiet. There is no greater symbol of that fear, I suppose, than the Walkman portable radio that you see pinching the heads of joggers and bicyclers, or the blaring radios that startle you awake when you line up beside cars at stoplights. You wonder when these noise addicts think—or whether they do. Are they afraid of silence? Are they afraid of being alone? I remember the words of Pascal, "All the evils of life have fallen upon us because men will not sit alone quietly in a room." How can God get in touch with them, if there is no quiet in their lives?

How admirable is the wisdom of a busy mother of a

large and poor family. A friend visiting her one day observed the room swarming with children. The friend
couldn't account for the fact that the mother was obviously
happy. How could she be, in such confusion? She never
had a moment alone. She had no quiet place in her one-
room house where she could retreat even for a brief moment to pray.

"It used to trouble me," she said, "until I found out the
secret. When things get too much for me, I just throw my
apron up over my head, and I am all alone with the Lord."

She should patent her discovery!

From my childhood I carry many happy memories.
None ranks higher than the one of the many hours I used
to spend along the creek down the road from our house.
There I could lose myself in contented exploration of the
world that lived in the shallow waters beneath the thick
bushes and trees. I've missed that creek. It gave me quiet.
Even a child needs it. Now I have to substitute something
like the mother's apron. The creek is gone, but the need
for solitude remains.

Let's return to Jesus. You recall the time when Jesus was
walking through a crowd so large it almost crushed Him,
and an unseen woman, who had been hemorrhaging for
twelve years, touched the edge of His garment. The Bible
says Jesus felt power go out from himself to her (Luke
8:46). Think, then, what it felt like for so many, many
people to receive healing from Him. How much power He
expended as He walked among the people! Is it any wonder that He had to get away to refuel? He had to draw
from the inexhaustible strength of His Father.

So do we.

I have worn out a couple of cars that have helped me
understand this need. They could hardly be more different. One is a little Dodge Colt, the ideal lightweight for
flitting around town. On the highway it can travel forty
miles on a gallon of gas. Four of us can squeeze into it if
we don't mind close fellowship. Not too comfortable, of
course, but we compensate for the crowded quarters by

laughing as we drive past gasoline stations.

The station wagon is another story. It's an eight-passenger Chevrolet, the last of the really big ones. Not infrequently we have filled it with people and then loaded the luggage rack on top (and mounted a loaded portable luggage carrier in front of that), and stuffed every crevice besides, and headed out. It doesn't quite average forty miles to the gallon. In fact, with that load it doesn't do much better than ten. Its heavier responsibilities demand that it stop much more frequently for refueling.

That's the reason for Jesus' frequent stops for fuel. His load was enormous. I suppose it is possible to flit through life, caring only for yourself, not pulling much of a load of service to the human race, with a shallow devotional life. But if you undertake some real ministries on behalf of the Lord, if you become involved with the needs and hurts of other people, you'll find you need to stop more often, refuel more frequently—and with a higher octane—than you used to.

Jesus did. So do we.

In the last chapter we discussed our need for regular Bible study. It is helpful to remember that prayer and Bible reading go together. Our meditation periods are conversations between God and ourselves; He speaks for a while (through His Word), we speak awhile, and we both listen.

Prayer

With this encouragement from Jesus' ministry, we turn to James 5:13-16, one of many Scriptures that exhort us to pray.

Is any one of you in trouble? He should pray. Is anyone happy? Let him sing songs of praise. Is any one of you sick? He should call the elders of the church to pray over him and anoint him with oil in the name of the Lord. And the prayer offered in faith will make the sick person well; the Lord will raise him up. If he has sinned, he will be forgiven. Therefore confess your sins to each other and pray for each other so that you may be healed. The prayer of a righteous man is powerful and effective.

It sounds incredible, doesn't it? But James draws on the words of Jesus himself: "If you remain in me and my words remain in you, ask whatever you wish, and it will be given you" (John 15:7).

The secret for us, of course, is whether we really have the close relationship with Jesus that powerful prayer requires. William Temple offers an instructive word here: "The proper outline of a Christian prayer is not 'Please do for me what I want.' It is 'Please do with me what You want.' That prayer will always be answered in proportion to its sincerity."[1]

"Powerful and effective" James calls the prayers of a righteous man. What then are some of the effects? What can we expect when we pray, if we pray in sincerity?

We can expect to be delivered from temptation. Jesus taught His disciples to pray, "And lead us not into temptation, but deliver us from the evil one" (Matthew 6:13). Then, when He struggled with the looming cross in the Garden of Gethsemane, Jesus urged His sleepy friends to "watch and pray so that you will not fall into temptation" (Matthew 26:41).

I appreciate these words because they come from one who the Bible says "has been tempted in every way, just as we are—yet was without sin" (Hebrews 4:15). When He tells us that prayer can keep us from succumbing to temptation, we can believe Him.

We can expect healing and the Lord's assistance in times of trouble. James urges us to pray when we are troubled and to elicit the prayers of our spiritual elders and brothers and sisters when we are sick. Can we expect to be helped when we pray? There is no other way to read this passage, is there? There is no other way to understand Jesus' promise (John 15:7), is there?

We can expect to be lined up with the will of God. Jesus taught us to pray, "Your kingdom come, your will be done on earth as it is in heaven" (Matthew 6:10). To pray this prayer is to begin with yourself: "Your will be done—in me!" "Your will be done—through me!" "Your will be done—by me!" "Let Your will and my will be always the same!"

We can expect to want God to be first in our lives. "Our Father in heaven, hallowed be your name' (Matthew 6:9). Christian prayer begins with devotion to God. We will have no other gods before Him (Exodus 20:3); we will love Him with everything we have (Matthew 22:37).

We can expect to become powerful. That is, full of power. This is what Jesus means by remaining in Him and having His words remain in us (John 15:7). It certainly is what Paul has in mind when he calls our bodies the temples of the Holy Spirit (1 Corinthians 6:19). They are to be kept holy because they are indwelt by the Spirit of Christ himself. Jesus informs His disciples what is in store for them when, before His ascension, He tells them, "You will receive power when the Holy Spirit comes on you" (Acts 1:8).

The apostle Paul's prayer for the Colossians (1:9-12) leaves no doubt that God's power is available if we but pray:

> Since the day we heard about you, we have not stopped praying for you and asking God to fill you with the knowledge of his will through all spiritual wisdom and understanding. And we pray this in order that you may live a life worthy of the Lord and may please him in every way: bearing fruit in every good work, growing in the knowledge of God, being strengthened with all power according to his glorious might so that you may have great endurance and patience.

What extravagant promises the Bible makes concerning our prayers! And I believe every one of them!

In what ways, then, shall we pray? Many answers could be given, but I hope these five will be enough to start you on your way to a regular, disciplined prayer life.

First, *pray in solitude.* I have said enough about this subject. I just mention it here to keep us from forgetting it.

Second, *pray in groups.* I have spoken so strongly about solitary prayer that I may have left the impression we have no need to pray in the company of others. I have done you a grievous injustice, if so. God created us to be in fellowship with others. We need the corporate prayer experiences of church worship. We need to pray also in small groups, like midweek Bible-study groups, home prayer groups, and Sunday-school classes. We need rich times of prayer with a special friend or confidant. We need to pray with our close loved ones.

Jesus often prayed alone. But often He took His close friends with Him. And He was faithful in His attendance at prayers in synagogues and temple. George Buttrick has incisively concluded, "For a man to argue, 'I do not go to church: I pray alone,' is no wiser than if he should say, 'I have no use for symphonies: I believe only in solo music.' Prayer is like life, for it is a life: it swings between the poles of aloneness and comradeship."[2]

Third, *pray in selfishness.* This seems a strange statement, perhaps, but I offer it as a necessary corrective for the many people who have told me, "I never pray for myself, only for others. It's selfish to pray for yourself."

It may be, but if so it is the kind of selfishness Jesus encourages. Didn't He teach us to ask for our daily bread, and pray to be kept out of temptation and delivered from evil? (Matthew 6:11-13).

If you are serious about living for Christ, if you really want to grow up as a Christian, you'll pray this prayer. You can't help it. You are so much aware of the distance between what you are and what you want to become that you'll not hesitate to ask the Lord's help in closing the gap.

You'll pray about other things, as well. You'll want the Lord's guidance in handling your finances, in deepening your relationships with others, in managing all your affairs in ways that will please Him.

Fourth, *you pray in intercession*. This word simply means that you pray earnestly for the needs of others. Here's a good example of the Bible's teaching on that:

> I urge, then, first of all, that requests, prayers, intercession and thanksgiving be made for everyone—for kings and all those in authority, that we may live peaceful and quiet lives in all godliness and holiness.
> —1 Timothy 2:1, 2

Even kings need our prayers! So do ministers. I take intercessory prayer very seriously, because I am convinced that my ministry has been sustained for a quarter of a century by quiet, godly people who have spoken to the Lord on my behalf all these years. I have returned the favor, and have reason to believe God has answered my prayers.

John Henry Jowett used to tell of a servant girl in his congregation many years ago who did not take her Christian life lightly. She was restricted in her church activities, however, because her work demanded almost all her time. She couldn't attend special meetings or even many of the regular church services. When her minister asked about her Christian life, she told him she always took the newspaper to bed with her at night.

When he asked what good that did, she told him that she would read the birth notices and pray for the new babies; then she would turn over to the death notices and pray for God's comfort to come into the sorrowing homes.

I wish she were in my church!

I suspect she is.

What I do know is that ours is a church family in which God's hand is seen in the lives of our members. They are praying for each other.

What joy you will experience when you begin regularly, fervently praying for others!

Fifth, *you pray in the Spirit*. Pray, in other words, without worrying about the correctness of your grammar or the limitations of your vocabulary. Pray even when you wonder whether you are making sense to God. Hang on to Romans 8:26: "We do not know what we ought to pray, but the Spirit himself intercedes for us with groans that words cannot express." The Spirit speaks for us, and God listens.

What more shall we say? I think Paul Scherer sums the subject up for us in one of his sermons. He discovered that in the Bible we are taught not to look around to see what we can make of life and then look up to God in prayer. When Moses took that approach, he killed a person! (Exodus 2:11, 12). Jesus' method was the opposite. He looked up first, then looked around (Luke 6:12, 13). He saved a world of persons!

Let's look up.

It will help us to grow up.

Discussion Starters for Small Groups

What is the greatest hindrance to your prayer life?

What has helped your prayer life the most?

Who do you know who has a powerful prayer life? How can you tell?

What is the relationship of confession and prayer?

To whom should you confess your sins?

How could your Christian friends help you grow in your prayer life?

CHAPTER TWELVE

Growing as a Spiritual Parent

─────────────

Ephesians 4:11-16

I like being a parent. I especially like being a parent during holiday seasons. This last Christmas was typical: all our natural-born kids were home, along with two of our "adopted" ones. The house seemed ready to burst with activity as they and their friends took over. What fun we had!

Grandma and Grandpa were here, too. They live in another state, so any visit with them is special. I couldn't help wondering if they shared something of my pride in seeing Joy's and my offspring (natural and otherwise) and their friends swarming the place. What a bunch they (and we) are responsible for!

When we are all together I often muse on what our children have done for me. Among other things, as I said earlier, they have made me better than I would have been without them. Because I have been responsible for them, I have not been free to indulge myself as I might otherwise have done. They have needed me to be reliable, upright,

and exemplary in my behavior. They have, in other words
brought out the best in me. They have kept me growing. It
has been good for me to be a parent.

To be a spiritual parent is equally beneficial. The Lord
intends for Christians to reproduce. That is not only the
way His kingdom grows on earth; it is also the way Christians
grow. Jesus stated it simply: "It is more blessed to
give than to receive." When we received Christ we were
indeed blessed; when we give Christ to someone else, the
blessing is incalculable! It is pleasing to receive a gift from
a wealthy donor, but this pleasure pales when compared
with the joy of being the donor giving the gifts.

The joy we receive when we give the best we have to
another is one of the things that compel us Christians to
share our faith. John states that his purpose in writing
what he knows about Jesus is "to make our joy complete"
(1 John 1:4). He can't keep the good news to himself.
Some manuscripts read "to make your joy complete," and
that is true also. Winning souls brings joy both to those
who are won and to those who win them.

Anthony Campolo tells of a missionary friend in Burma
who was preaching on a street corner one day to a very
hostile crowd. They tried to shout him down, interrupting
his sermon with hoots and catcalls. He was about to give
up in frustration when a Buddhist monk came by and
silenced the crowd. "Listen to this man," he shouted.
"Don't you know *he needs* to tell you about his God?"[1]

That's the truth, but for a reason the monk may not have
fully understood. He probably thought the man had to
preach because his God was insisting on it. It is true that
God expects us to tell the good news to others, of course.
But one wonders whether the Buddhist monk could have
realized the missionary's hope that he might persuade another
to accept Jesus Christ, and thus have the same wonderful
new life he enjoys. Could the monk have known
what it is like to be a spiritual parent? Could he have had
any idea of how a Christian grows when he is involved in
reproducing, in making additional Christians?

A very famous Scripture (Ephesians 4:11-16) clearly illustrates the close relationship between reproducing and personal growth. God has given the church apostles, prophets, evangelists, pastors and teachers, this passage teaches, so that God's people in the church can be prepared to do their part in helping it to grow. They are to help each other become united and knowledgeable and mature in Christ. When the church functions like a body, with each part doing its work, the whole body grows larger (has more members) and each member grows up as well. The movement of the passage is from the growth of the church as a whole into a larger and better body, to the personal growth of each member as each one does his or her part to help the whole.

God's design, the book of Ephesians states, is to unite the whole world in Christ. The church's job, then, is to carry this good news to every alienated person on earth. The Christian's task is to help the church reach these people. The Christian's blessing is that each act of reaching the separated ones helps the Christian grow up.

How then can we help? What do we have to do to become spiritual parents, helping others to become born again? We can answer three questions.

What Do I Have to Give?

We all have the same thing to give: good news. When the angel appeared to the shepherds watching their flocks on the night Jesus was born, he gave the same thing we give: "Do not be afraid. I bring you *good news.*" That's what the gospel is: good news from God.

It is this good news that makes spiritual parenting so easy. When you love another person, you give the best you have. What is best about a Christian's life is the fact that Christ has saved him from his sins, adopted him into the family of God, prepared a place in eternity for him, and thus given him everything to live for. That's good news. And that's shareable good news. Not only does the Christian lose nothing of what he has when he shares it with another, but he can only fully appreciate what he has in Christ by sharing it. He may be giving it away, but he gains more in the giving than he would have in the keeping. I learned a bit about this from Herbert J. Taylor, a dynamic Christian businessman who played a significant role in several Christian organizations as well as in the Rotary Club. Early in his years as an insurance salesman, he was complaining over dinner about one of his contacts who failed to buy life insurance from him. His wife listened patiently, but she didn't accept his self-pity. She asked him two questions: Does the man really need insurance, and does he have enough money to pay the premiums? Taylor answered yes to both questions.

"You know what I think?" she then asked him. "I think you are to blame for not selling him the policy. It's not his fault for not buying." (Nothing like a good wife to make us feel better about ourselves!)

Taylor accepted his wife's criticism. He realized that he had something the man really needed. He had just not made a persuasive enough presentation. He went back to the man and sold him a ten-thousand-dollar policy. It was a turnaround in his career. In the previous six months he had sold only a hundred thousand dollars' worth of life insurance; in the next six months he sold more than six hundred thousand dollars' worth and began winning awards for his top salesmanship.[2] What made the difference? He became sold on the worth of his product and on his responsibility to convince others that they needed what he had found.

He had something to give. So do you and I. We have the best news this world has ever heard. We have the solution to the baffling problems of our crazy times. We know how to put broken families back together again, how to mend broken dreams, how to give ruined lives a fresh start, how to introduce despairing people to love, joy, and peace. We know all this. Isn't it wrong of us to sit on our knowledge? If the world is ignoring God, whose fault is it? If people have turned cynical about the church, whom should they criticize? Can they be blamed if we have the good news and aren't sharing it?

Chuck White made the headlines when he saved two lives in forty-eight hours. He was on two-week reserve duty at Fort Gordon. A nursing aide at a psychiatric ward in Miami, White was assigned as an assistant in the Family Practice unit at Fort Gordon's Eisenhower Memorial Center. He had just left the floor to get a prescription when he stepped outside for a quick cigarette. Hearing a lady's screams, he rushed to where her little girl was choking. Other people were walking by, but no one was helping. White tried to remove what was in the girl's throat and, failing that, he turned her over and applied the Heimlich maneuver. After White applied two thrusts just below her sternum, a piece of hard candy popped out, and the girl, who was already turning blue, began to breathe normally.

The next day White was watching a platoon running by when one of the men fell out. Several other men kneeled over him as he choked and threw up. Quickly White turned him on his back and cleared his air passage. The recruit was then admitted to the Medical Center with a respiratory infection that officials said could very well have killed him if he hadn't had immediate attention.

Base officials credited Chuck White with saving both lives by his quickness of mind and his competency.[3]

What interests me is that in both instances, there were several others who could have stepped in to help before White got there. But they didn't. Some probably didn't know what to do. Others didn't want to get involved. But White, who had earlier taught himself how to administer the Heimlich maneuver and CPR therapy, cared enough about these people in need to help them.

Or should I say, he cared enough about people in the first place to learn how to help them if an emergency should ever arise?

How much do you and I care? Enough to learn how to tell other people the good news about the Savior of mankind? Enough to become a youth sponsor, a Sunday-school teacher, a nursery worker, a helpful neighbor, a constant friend? Enough to think more about giving than receiving? You have good news to give! So do I.

How Then Can I Give It?

God has given us the good news to give. More than that, He has also made it possible for every believer to help get the good news out. Remember the final clause of Ephesians 4:11-16? " . . . as each part does its work." The apostle Paul returns again and again to his picture of the church as a body and each member as a contributing member:

> Just as each of us has one body with many members, and these members do not all have the same function, so in Christ we who are many form one body, and each member belongs to all the others. We have different gifts, according to the grace given us. If a man's gift is prophesying, let him use it in proportion to his faith. If it is serving, let him serve; if it is teaching, let him teach; if it is encouraging, let him encourage; if it is contributing to the needs of others, let him give generously; if it is leadership, let him govern diligently; if it is showing mercy, let him do it cheerfully.
> —Romans 12:4-8; see also 1 Corinthians 12:7-11

How do you do your part in getting the good news to the people who need it? By dedicating your own spiritual gift or gifts, your talents and abilities, to the work of the church—and being certain that your church is fulfilling the assignment the Lord has given to make disciples of everyone (Matthew 28:18-20). By seizing every opportunity to speak a word for the Lord. By starting where you are.

Jesus one time gave His disciples an unforgettable lesson in fishing. He had been teaching a large crowd from a boat at the edge of the Sea of Galilee. When He had finished, He told Simon Peter to "put out into deep water and let down the nets for a catch."

Simon protested, "Master, we've worked hard all night and haven't caught anything. But because you say so, I will let down the nets."

When he obeyed Jesus, he hauled in a catch so large he had to signal to another boat for help. His success nearly submerged his boat. Overwhelmed by what had happened, Peter fell at Jesus' knees and said, "Go away from me, Lord; I am a sinful man."

Jesus calmed his fears and challenged his future at the same time. "Don't be afraid; from now on you will catch men" (Luke 5:1-11). As always, Jesus' real concern was for people. His moral? Obey the Lord and go where the people are. Seize your opportunities to "catch" them for Him.

Jesus walked among the multitudes to bring good news to them in the form of teaching, preaching, and healing. He sent (and still sends) His disciples to similar multitudes for the same purpose. When the Lord looks at crowds, He does not, like a wily businessman, see a market to be exploited; nor like an ambitious employer, see laborers to be used; nor like crafty politicians, count the votes to be garnered. He sees sheep without a shepherd, the sick without physicians, the ignorant without teachers, the lost without a savior. He sees opportunities everywhere.

He has commissioned a church to take the good news to the multitudes; He has constructed His church so that every member can make a special contribution to the church's purpose.

Sometimes the action is dramatic, like the sacrificial effort of a foreign missionary laboring in a hostile or primitive culture. Sometimes it seems small, even insignificant, but has lasting effect. Becky Manley Pippert, for example, tells in her *Out of the Saltshaker* of a symbolic statement an elderly Christian made in a well-dressed middle-class church in Portland, Oregon.

The story begins with a brilliant but eccentric university student. His uniform gave him away: perpetually uncombed hair, unkempt and unmatched clothes, no shoes. He lived on the edge of social acceptability. Then one day he became a Christian. Drawn to the proper, socially self-conscious church across from the campus, he decided to worship there one Sunday morning. When he walked down the aisle in his blue jeans, tee shirt, and bare feet, an uncomfortable hush descended over the congregation. His was a long walk, since the church was crowded and he had to make his way to the very front to find a seat. When he reached the front he found every seat taken, so he did the natural thing—for him, not for the proper church—of squatting on the carpet. The congregation was unnerved. Tension filled the air.

It quickly thickened as an old man left his seat and walked with some difficulty down the aisle. Was he going to scold the young man? Was he going to invite him out?

They watched as, surprisingly, he sat down next to him on the carpet, not an easy task for a man his age. There he remained for the hour, uniting with the young man in worship.

In that simple act he reached out to the newcomer with friendship, acceptance, and love. It was the start of his spiritual parenting. He seized the opportunity and acted out the good news without having to utter a word.

It is not difficult to meet the needs of those you love. You just take what you have—your abilities and talents, your God-given gifts, your money and time, your quiet influence—and place it at the disposal of your loved ones. You just forget yourself for the sake of another.

Following a strenuous board meeting of the Christian Missionary Fellowship one evening, I turned down an invitation to attend a board party at a member's home because I was under some pressure to complete a writing assignment. After an hour or two of writing in my motel room, however, my mind quit, so I turned on the television set for some relaxation. A Jack Lemmon movie, "Missing," was showing. I was quickly captivated by this thriller. Set in the midst of a Latin-American revolution, the movie traced the desperate effort of a wife and father to locate their missing husband and son.

The wife and father misunderstood each other but were held together in their unflinching determination to do anything, to make any sacrifice, to press every opportunity, to find their lost loved one. What were they willing to give? Everything they had! They would risk everything in order to save his life.

What do you have to give in seeking the lost? Everything God has given you.

How do you give it? By forgetting yourself in your love.

Then What's in It for Me?

We don't easily hear this talk of self-sacrifice in religion. It sounds foreign, super-pious, to the secular ear.

If this makes you uncomfortable, then let me take you back to the joy of parenting. All effective parents have learned that there is no success in child-rearing apart from some definite sacrificing on their part. I do not mean that parents surrender their individuality or authority; that way lies disaster. But because they have children, they do sacrifice some of their freedoms and dreams in order to do what is in the best interests of their children. They really don't think of their acts as sacrificial; they just do what is expected of people who love their children.

That's all spiritual parents do. You simply do what's best for your spiritual offspring, or for those you want to bring into the family. There are few heroics involved.

Jasper Brown, a nineteen-year-old former Largo High School football player, was lauded by his community for climbing through the window of a neighbor's burning house to rescue an eight-year-old boy. He even received a letter of commendation from President Reagan. It would have been easy for the young man to be carried away by all this attention. But Brown offered a balanced response to all this attention. "All that matters to me is that Robert was saved."[4]

That's all that matters to spiritual parents as well.

But we have to admit that the rewards of spiritual parenting are typical of the lavish blessings God pours out on those who love Him. The spiritual parent enjoys rich friendship with the other members of the family of God, a fellowship so rewarding that it seems incredible there should be anything more.

There is more, though. The parenting Christian feels himself growing into a stronger, wiser person. I like what Paul Tournier has written on this subject. He insists that the Christian life keeps its fervor only through ministering. Even the Christian who feels too inadequate to share his faith or serve another in Christ's name must do so, Tournier argues. To the person who hesitates to minister because he hasn't solved all his personal problems, he says such a person might be excused if what were required were teaching or preaching, since these are the vocation of specially trained leaders.

> For us ordinary believers, it is just when we are aware of our inadequacy, and feel that we are morally no better than those who come to us, that we can help them the most.[5]

We help them—and ourselves. Our involvement in taking others to the Lord who cares about our problems effects a change in our attitudes, which is another of the great rewards of introducing other people to Christ. No longer can we be charged with chanting,

> "We're among the saved;
> You're among the damned.
> There's room for you in Hell,
> We don't want Heaven crammed."

We'll not look at people the way we once did. We'll see instead with the eyes of God, who wants the whole world saved.

We'll become more like the father of a soldier who was in the crowd of parents at the railroad station seeing their sons off to war. Someone called out as the train pulled away from the station, "Boys, give them hell." Immediately this father shouted to his boy, "Son, give them Christ."

That's what's in it for you. You'll begin to think of saving, not of killing; of blessing, not of beating; of loving, not of hating. You'll have in you the mind of Christ, who humbled himself to rescue the lost.

John Greenlee has captured the love of God in his little parable of the man standing before Heaven's gate. He couldn't get through, because the gatekeeper blocked his way.

"Will the others be along soon?" the gatekeeper asked.

Puzzled by the question, the pilgrim stood silent for a moment. "Others? I ah I'm not sure I understand . . . what others do you mean?"

"The ones you have brought to this place," replied the gatekeeper. "The others whom you asked to join you here; the people in earth-life whom you invited to the Heaven-life in Christ . . . will they be along soon?"

As they were talking, a mother and her children arrived, and the gatekeeper let them pass immediately through the gate. Then two businessmen arrived, the one having been invited by the other. The gatekeeper gave them ready access to the way into Heaven.

Then he spoke again to the pilgrim. "Sir, there are no restrictions about who may enter here. Whosoever will may come in. But no one has ever entered alone. For if you are alone here in eternity-life, then surely that which you held as faith in the earth-life was not worthy or compelling enough to share with someone else. I don't mean to be difficult about this business, but surely you see that Heaven-life is a matter of shared love and deep fellowship in the faith we have together in Jesus Christ. It just isn't a place where one would want to be alone. The very air we breathe in Heaven-life is filled with shared love. You would have great difficulty even breathing if you are alone."

The pilgrim offered the usual excuses—too busy, too

preoccupied to share his knowledge of eternity-life with anyone else. He said, "Well I did think about it once in a while about inviting someone else to worship with me. But I was always so busy all week and felt like I'd done my best just to get to worship myself. I never thought inviting someone else was a big deal . . . nothing serious. I had my own salvation and I figured the next guy would have to look out for himself. He knew where the church building was. So . . . I guess I didn't get around to asking anyone else."

The gatekeeper was astonished that in a lifetime the pilgrim never had even a few minutes to tell somebody else the most important news the world has ever heard.

Finally he broke the silence. "There is no record of anyone ever having entered this gate alone. I will have to ask the Master. But I can say that it is a most unusual situation . . . strange that you could have been given so much . . . and kept it all for yourself. I will have to ask Him . . . most unusual."[6]

And most self-defeating. Jesus warned a long time ago that the person who tries to save *his* life will lose it (Matthew 10:39). A paradox of the Christian faith is that only by giving it away can you be assured of having it.

May I take you back one more time to my family room? There are Mom and Dad and the kids. And their friends. It is a noisy place, a sometimes chaotic place. But when I think what it would be like if there were no children, then I realize how much wealth they have brought to me.

And when I meet in our church building with my family in Christ, I spot the ones I have influenced in one way or another who have now become a part of the family of God; when I contemplate an eternity together with this family, then I am ready for the question, "What's in it for me to become a spiritual parent?"

The answer is, "Everything!"

Discussion Starters for Small Groups

In what ways is the church unlike a service club?

What is the function of leaders in the church?

What is the function of members?

What is the goal of the church?

What is the result of reaching that goal?

How is your local congregation similar to (or different from) the model described by Paul in Ephesians 4?

Why is it important that every Christian be involved in active ministry?

How can you personally help your congregation achieve the goal stated in Ephesians 4?

CHAPTER THIRTEEN

The Final Test:
How Tough Is Your Love?

Luke 6:27-36

In the same week, two news stories did something quite unusual for the secular press: they riveted their readers' attention on Christian doctrine.

The first appeared in the Phoenix *Republic* for January 6, 1984. Accompanied by a three-column photo of Walter and Dawn Beall and their two little children, the news article recounted their narrow escape from death the previous July.

It happened when Dawn's sister and two friends moved to Arizona from Pennsylvania. The three of them spent several weeks at the Bealls' home until they found a rental house. Then, after their pickup truck broke down, the trio moved back into the Bealls' house on July 23 to be close to a construction site where Dawn's sister's boyfriend worked.

The boyfriend spent that discouraging day drinking, feeling sorry for himself because of the auto breakdown, his girlfriend's refusal to requite his love, and the low pay of his construction job. Suddenly, at 5:15 p.m. he went crazy. He stabbed Dawn Beall and her four-month-old baby. He chased Walter Beall's mother with the hunting knife. Then he went into the bedroom where Walter was sleeping and stabbed him several times.

When the police officer arrived, he thought Walter was dead, but paramedics labored over him, breaking his ribs in order to revive him. The assailant had stabbed him in the chest, left leg, and right arm, leaving the right arm permanently crippled.

The madman also stabbed Mrs. Beall twice in the chest, with one wound slicing through the aorta, the main artery from the heart. Twice she almost died in the hospital. The child lost one-sixth of a kidney after being stabbed in the back.

The police apprehended Bernard Devine and jailed him.

So far the story reads like another gruesome crime story. But now it becomes very different. The article headline reads "The Other Cheek"; and the subheading continues, "Victims' leniency plea is ignored." Walter and Dawn Beall stood before the bench to beg the judge to be merciful to Bernard Devine in spite of the fact that he nearly killed them.

Their plea went ignored. They weren't asking for no punishment at all; just for leniency. But everyone in the courtroom was stunned by the victims' behavior. The prosecutor said he had "never, never seen anything like this. Someone who is brutally attacked—stabbed—to come in and plead for mercy? I'm flabbergasted."

The Bealls' explanation was right out of Luke 6:27-36. "If we can show love and forgiveness to some person that's hurt us," they said, "then maybe someone else can do the same. Our world needs something like that—if people could only forgive."

When they heard that the judge gave Devine a thirty-year sentence, Dawn Beall said, "That's a shame. Jesus Christ forgave every one of us for what we did. If He could forgive our sins, I guess I have to (forgive Devine)."[1]

The day after reading this article I received *Time* for January 9, 1984. The cover photo was of Pope John Paul II and Mehmet Ali Agca, the man who tried to assassinate the pope two years earlier. John Paul was shaking Agca's hand and comforting him with his left hand on his would-be-assassin's shoulder. In bold letters the news-magazine asked, "Why forgive?"

John Paul II had just visited the Rome jail holding Agca prisoner. Dismissing any audience, the pope stayed in the convict's cell for over twenty minutes. While there, he again forgave Agca for the shooting, repeating the pardon he had given him immediately after the attempted assassination.

The *Time* writer was moved by this prison meeting, saying that "the meaning of John Paul's forgiveness was profoundly Christian. He embraced his enemy and pardoned him." For most of his long article, the writer, Lance Morrow, struggled with the relevance of the Christian doctrine of forgiveness to world problems. He said it "sometimes makes sense as sentiment, but not as social policy." Yet, after weighing justice and mercy and the claims of God and Caesar, he had to conclude, "Forgiveness does not look much like a tool for survival in a bad world. But that is what it is."[2]

Is it possible that Jesus is not just offering pious talk in Luke 6:27-36? Is His teaching, which seems so unattainably idealistic, actually the only practical way to solve world and personal problems? Did He, in condensing all Old Testament rules into the two overriding principles of love for God and love for neighbor (Matthew 22:34-40) give us the only key to survival?

Further, Jesus is obviously not blind to how tough love must be. He does not present love as a first step in spiritual growth. It is rather the final test. It has to be stronger than anything else. Love, as Paul reminds us in 1 Corinthians 13, never quits. Only love is powerful enough to pardon the man who tries to kill you.

Look at the tough cases Jesus expects our love to win:

"Love your enemies."
"Do good to those who hate you."
"Bless those who curse you."
"Pray for those who mistreat you."
"Turn the other cheek."
"Give more than is asked of you."
"Do to others as you would have them do to you."

Then, to be certain we don't misunderstand, Jesus repeats himself in verses 32-36. As always, He calls our attention to the character of God. If your love is this tough, "you will be sons of the Most High, because he is kind to the ungrateful and wicked." We are to imitate God: "Be merciful, just as your Father is merciful."

As we meditate on this incredibly demanding passage, an unexpected truth takes hold of us. We have always thought that growth and maturity would strengthen our defenses, keep us from getting hurt. People wouldn't "get to us" the way they did when we were younger. Children admire their parents because they seem so strong, so in command. Little children have trouble believing that their parents have feelings, too, or are hurt sometimes. When the little fellow boasts, "My daddy can lick your daddy," he believes it. To a child, being adult means to be able to take charge, to be stronger than anybody else, to not get hurt.

Jesus gives us a whole new definition of maturity and tough love, doesn't He? The child now brags, "My daddy *won't* lick your daddy." Maturity's final test is love, and love's toughness is of an absorbing kind. It does not meet the neighborhood bully with doubled fists. It doesn't beat up enemies; it loves them. It doesn't return hate for hate, evil for evil, but responds with good. Love does not curse the curser, or mistreat the mistreater, or hit the hitter, or do as little as possible, Instead, it gives more than is asked of it. It loves with a love like God's.

Love risks being hurt. During World War II, the wife of an English Royal Air Force officer lived every day with the knowledge that her husband might be killed in an air battle. So when he was granted an unexpected brief leave in London to be with his wife and three small children before going on a dangerous mission, she prepared a celebration. Leaving him at home with the children, she went shopping for what groceries she could get for the feast in wartime London. While she was at the shops, however, a sudden daytime bombing raid hit the city. Her house was destroyed and her husband and three children were killed.

The grieving widow suppressed her sorrow in her effort to help her country and her neighbors through the war. In time another man, of whom she had grown very fond, asked her to marry him. She couldn't give an immediate answer. She had loved before—loved a man, loved her children. And she had lost them all. She was afraid to try it again. So many risks, so much hurt. How much safer to remain single, to protect herself from the pain and sacrifice of love. Then, summoning all her courage, she took the risk.[3] Love with the risk of being hurt was more important than security without love. Loving again would be dangerous, but only by facing the danger could she find fullness of life.

It is the openness to danger that William Manchester writes about in his memoir of the Pacific theater of World War II. Hospitalized by a serious wound he sustained when his company was under heavy fire, Manchester chafed under his confinement until he couldn't stand it any longer. Violating his orders, he returned to join his buddies at the front even though his decision meant almost certain death.

But he didn't die, and thirty-five years later he still pondered that decision. He could have stayed in the hospital. He didn't have to leave that security to face the guns. He was under orders not to. Yet he went. It was, he said, "an act of love." He had come to view those men at the front as his family. They had fought together, survived together, and they had not let him down. He couldn't desert them either. "I had to be with them, rather than let them die and me live with the knowledge that I might have saved them.... Any man in combat who lacks comrades who will die for him, or for whom he is willing to die, is not a man at all. He is," Manchester adds, "truly damned."[4]

Involvement, risk, vulnerability, hurt, willingness to die—these are the companions of love. These are not "religious" sounding words, are they? I recall wondering one time what it would feel like to love people the way Jesus loved them. A good insight came from an older minister who answered the same question for a younger one. "Well, I don't think you'd ever know. Because if you were loving people the way Jesus loved them, you wouldn't be thinking about how you were feeling. You'd be totally absorbed in the other person's problem."[5]

The older man's answer is wisdom itself. True love wraps itself up in another. It is far, far from the self-consciousness of a young student who was much more scientific than romantic. His relationship with a special young woman was progressing quite nicely when all of a sudden she dropped him. She had discovered that while he was whispering sweet nothings in her ear, he was, to test her reactions to his ardor, carefully keeping his finger on her pulse.

True love is never so self-conscious; nor is it especially religious. In fact, the demanding words of Jesus we are studying here say nothing about feeling religious. He asks that we act, not feel. The final test of Christian maturity is not whether you feel more religious or not, but whether you act more loving!

Reading some of the religious documents of Buddhism a few years ago helped me to understand Jesus' teaching on love a little better. Several of my students, wanted to learn more about Eastern religions, since these were making a splash among the "in" crowds in America then. I was especially fascinated by the treatment of love in the four *Brahma viharas*. There is *metta*, which is lovingkindness, or love between equals. Then there is *karuna*, compassion, the love of a superior for an inferior. Then *mudita*, love that reaches upward, the love of an inferior for a superior, of the person who has little for the person who has much. Then there is the highest love of all, *upekkha*, a detached, impersonal love that makes no distinctions of higher or lower; it acts the same toward people of great benevolence as to people given to criminal violence.

That's the best Buddhism offers—indifference.

I turned with eagerness back to the Christian faith, where the highest love is agape, which is love that loves even when there is no love in return. It is more. It is love that drives money changers out of the temple, love that gives sight back to the blind and hearing back to the deaf, love that casts out demons, love that does not lash back when it is lashed, love that refuses to call down the wrath of God upon people who deserve it, love that does not run away from Gethsemane in a night of agony, love that goes to the cross. It is, above all, love that cares. Buddha may remain indifferent; Christ cannot. Buddha may be untouched by the battle; Christ gets himself bloodied trying to rescue His buddies, and His buddies are many.

This agape is always, inescapably, an act of will above dependence on mere feeling.

It acts lovingly even when the feeling is gone. A popular newspaper columnist in the Midwest, Dr. George Crane, once told of a woman who came to his office spouting hatred for her husband. She not only wanted to get rid of him, she told Dr. Crane, but she wanted to get even! Her goal was to hurt him as much as she could before she divorced him because of what he had done to her.

Dr. Crane agreed to help. He devised a plan for her. She should go home and act as if she really loved him. She should tell him how much he meant to her, praising all his good qualities, mentioning every decent trait. She should go out of her way to be as kind, generous, and considerate as possible. She should do whatever was necessary to convince him of her undying love. Then, when she had convinced him, she could drop the bomb about divorce.

When she then told him how much she hated him, it would really hurt him.

That was just the advice she was looking for. She went home and eagerly put the plan into effect. She would act "as if" she loved him. That would show him!

She was a good actress. The plan succeeded. But when it was time for her to return to Dr. Crane, she didn't show up. So Crane called her. "Are you ready now to go through with the divorce?"

"Divorce?" she exclaimed. "Never! I discovered I really do love him."[6]

Dr. Crane demonstrated a basic truth of the Christian doctrine of love. Love is something you do, not merely something you feel. A forty-seven-year-old housewife, married twenty-seven of those years and the mother of six children, has as clear-eyed a view of marital love as you can find: "Love is what you've been through with somebody." It acts.

But it acts out of a previously adopted principle; it results from an earlier decision that the person loving will act toward, not just react to, the person loved. Christian love takes charge of the lover. A loving Christian is thus not tossed about by whims, fads, impulses, desires, lusts, angers, drives. A Christian is not at the mercy of enemies or haters or cursers or somebody who mistreats him. He has chosen to love; he will love in spite of the behavior of the one he loves. Love is an act of will.

Corrie ten Boom recalls with tenderness her mother's last three years on earth. Paralyzed by a stroke, she could scarcely make her body do anything, yet Corrie says it was astonishing to see the quality of life her mother was able to lead in her crippled body. Hers had always been an active love, expressing itself through her soup pot and sewing basket. Now she couldn't make soup or sew for her neighbors. She could remember, though, and she could communicate with Corrie so that her daughter could convey her messages.

Corrie would know when Mrs. ten Boom was thinking

of someone's birthday. Then Corrie would call out names until the older woman would say "Yes." And Corrie would write a little note saying that her Mama had seen the person from her house window and wished her a happy birthday. Mrs. ten Boom would then scrawl her barely legible signature. The paralyzed saint was soon known all over her Dutch city of Haarlem for her kind birthday notes.

All she could do was sit in her chair by her window — and love. She taught Corrie, her daughter wrote, "that love is larger than the walls which shut it in.''[7] There's much more to say about our Christian growth and development and about love as the final test of our maturity. But the pages of this book are running out, so I must quit.

You must be disappointed that I have not offered Ten Easy Steps to Spiritual Perfection on these pages. I wish I knew them. But, as I've said all along, we don't use the term "growing pains" for nothing. Growth is painful, time-consuming, energy-depleting, mind-stretching — and soul-filling. The world is full of men and women who somewhere in their past, made the decision not to grow up. They may be wrinkled and gray by now, but inwardly they have remained children. We know them well — we have to take care of them.

Jesus has urged us to *become* like children, at the same time giving every assistance so that we will not *remain* children indefinitely. Childlikeness is the goal, not childishness.

I hope these pages have been faithful to His teaching. I also hope every chapter will help you, as the writing of it has helped me, to do what it takes to grow up into Christ. He alone is a worthy model. He is what God had in mind when He created humanity. The fully developed and mature person, then, will look like Jesus.

Discussion Starters for Small Groups

Who are your enemies?

What does Jesus say you should do to those who seek to harm you?

What does Jesus say is to be your motivation for responding in this way?

Describe a time when you forgave someone who wronged you. Why did you forgive? What was the result?

In Luke 6:27-36, does love seem like an emotion? Why or why not?

What is the significance of this?

Give a testimony of God's mercy toward you this week?

What can you do this week to show mercy to others?

End Notes

Introduction:
1. Quoted in Time, July 4, 1983, p. 66.
2. New York: The Macmillan Company, 1960, p. 174.

Chapter 1:
1. "Whatever Happened to Humility?" Christian Standard (August 29, 1982), p. 12.
2. Ronald W. Clark, Benjamin Franklin, A Biography (New York: Random House, Co., 1983), pp. 19, 20.
3. E. Stanley Jones, Christ at the Round Table (The Abingdon Press, Co, 1928), p. 192.
4. Gwen Bagni, and Paul Dubov, Backstairs at the White House (New Jersey: Prentice-Hall, Co., 1978), p. 464.

Chapter 2:
1. Markings (New York: Alfred A. Knopf, 1964), p. 124.
2. Waco, Texas: Word Books, Co., 1982, p. 85.
3. The Healing of Persons (New York: Harper and Row, Publishers, Co., 1965), p. 167.

Chapter 3:
1. September 16, 1983.
2. Maisie Ward, Gilbert Keith Chesterton (Sheed and Ward, 1943), p. 60.
3. Quoted in Karl Menninger, Whatever Became of Sin (New York: Hawthorn Books, Inc., 1973), p. 198.
4. "The Electronic Church," Missouri in Perspective (March 27, 1978), p. 5.

Chapter 4:
1. Locked in a Room with Open Doors (Waco, Texas: Word Publishing Company, 1974), p. 117.
2. Quoted in Reader's Digest (January 1980), p. 71.
3. B. A. Botkin, A Civil War Treasury of Tales, Legends and Folklore (New York: Promontory Press, Co., 1960).
4. Robert Schuller, Self Esteem, the New Reformation (Waco: Word Books, Co., 1982), pp. 102-103.
5. "Peter Rose: A Ball Player with Hustle," Arizona Republic Gazette (Sunday, October 19, 1980).

Chapter 5:
1. Leadership (Spring Quarter 1983), p. 93.
2. William Barclay, Ethics in a Permissive Society (New York: Harper and Row, Co., 1971), p. 111.
3. Marshall Hayden, "Oh, the Temptation!" Christian Standard (August 27, 1978), pp. 4, 5.
4. Stanley Mooneyham of World Vision. Quoted by Russell Blowers, "Minister's Memo," The 91st Editor (May 1, 1981).
5. Time (March 25, 1974), pp. 42, 43.
6. Time (February 7, 1983), p. 64.

Chapter 6:
1. Time (June 6, 1983), p. 48.
2. The Adventure of Living, tr. Edwin Hudson (New York: Harper and Row, Publishers, 1963), p 123.
3. George MacDonald, an Anthology, ed. C. S. Lewis (Fount Paperbacks Co., 1946), p. 58.
4. Letters and Papers from Prison, the Enlarged Edition, ed. Eberhard Bethge (New York: The Macmillan Company, 1972), p. 114.
5. Antoine de Saint-Exupery, Wind, Sand and Stars (New York: Time Reading Program, Co., 1939), p. 18.

Chapter 7:
1. The Kern Park Christian (November 18-24, 1962).
2. Alvin Dark, "Stewardship" The Christian Athlete (November, 1962), p. 2.

Chapter 8:
1. Reported in Evangelical Newsletter (July 10, 1981).
2. Paul E. Larson, Wise Up and Live (Glendale: Regal Books Division, Gospel Light Pub., 1971), pp. 130, 131.

Chapter 9:
1. New York: Avon Books, Co., 1971, p. 354.
2. Time (October 26, 1978), p. 129.
3. Reading for Pleasure, ed. Bennett Cerf (New York: Harper and Brothers, Co., 1957), p. 525.
4. Masie Ward, Gilbert Keith Chesterton (Sheed and Ward, 1943), p. 159.
5. Stephen Board, "Inventory Day, November 27," Eternity (November, 1980), p. 5.

Chapter 10:
1. Collins (Fontana Books, London, Co. 1969), p. 37.

2. "A Layman and His Faith," Christianity Today (October 10, 1960), p. 23.
3. Leroy Elms, The Lost Art of Disciple Making (Grand Rapids: Zondervan Publishing House, 1978), p. 61.
4. Kenneth Chafin, Help! I'm a Layman (Waco, Texas: Word Books, Co., 1966), pp. 46-47.

Chapter 11:
1. Daily Readings from William Temple (London: Hodder and Stoughton, St. Paul House), p. 8.
2. Prayer (New York: Abingdon Press, 1942), p. 35.

Chapter 12:
1. A Reasonable Faith (Waco: Word Books, Co., 1983), p. 9.
2. The Herbert J. Taylor Story (Illinois: Intervarsity Press, Co., 1968), pp. 31, 32.
3. E. Ray Jones, "Minister Muses," Clearwater Christian (September 26, 1979).
4. Again I am indebted to Ray Jones. "Minister Muses," Clearwater Christian (April 20, 1983).
5. The Person Reborn (London: SCM Press, Ltd., 1967), pp. 215-216.
6. Conejo Caller (January 30, 1980).

Chapter 13:
1. Laurie Roberts, Republic staff (January 6, 1984).
2. Time (January 9, 1984), p. 28.
3. Madeleine L'Engle, Walking on Water (Illinois: Harold Shaw Publishers, Co., 1980), pp. 192, 193.
4. Goodbye, Darkness (Toronto: Little, Brown, and Company, Co., 1979), p. 391.
5. Keith Miller, Bruce Larson, Carriers of the Spirit (Waco: Word Books, 1979), p. 114.
6. J. Allan Peterson, The Mythe of the Greener Grass (Wheaton: Tyndale House Publishers, Co., 1983), p. 200.
7. The Hiding Place (Minneapolis: Special Film Edition, World Wide Pictures), pp. 67, 68.